Cooking the Middle Eastern Way

Eat together and do not eat separately,
for the blessing is with the company.
Hadith, or saying of the Prophet Muhammad.

This book was devised and produced by
Multimedia Publications (UK) Ltd

Editor: Anthony Lambert
Production: Arnon Orbach
Design: Megra Mitchell,
    John Strange and Associates
Photography: Theo Bergström
    and Christine Osborne

First published in the United States of
America 1985 by

CHARTWELL BOOKS, INC.
A Division of **BOOK SALES, INC.**
110 Enterprise Avenue
Secaucus, New Jersey 07094

ISBN 0-89009-838-7

Origination by D.S. Colour International Ltd,
    London
Typeset by Flowery Typesetters Ltd
Printed in Italy

Cooking the Middle Eastern Way

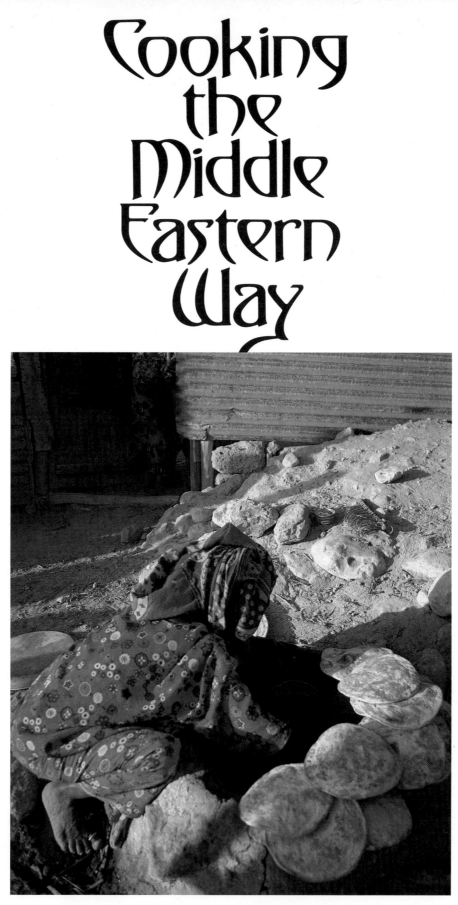

Christine Osborne

CHARTWELL BOOKS, INC.

Contents

A mezze table, in Beirut.

Fruits in Jericho, West Bank.

Spices in the attarine or spice street, Muharraq, Bahrain.

Ripening dates in the Shatt al-Arab delta, Iraq.

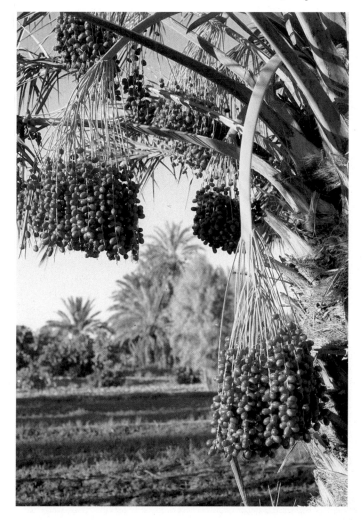

Foreword

As you might imagine, I had many adventures in my endeavors to learn the secrets of Middle Eastern cooking.

Most unusual was a lunch in North Yemen in a restaurant no bigger than a large hole in the wall. This is precisely what it was, a cavity in the wall around the capital, Sana'a, into which an enterprising Yemeni had maneuvered some tables and chairs.

I had not finished eating when the space was invaded by crowds of men who, unable to squeeze past, walked across the top of my table. Then, finding a seat, they unclipped daggers and hung them on a hook as a Westerner might his umbrella. No one paid me, the only woman, the slightest attention. As far as they knew, I might have been a *djinn!*

Quite the opposite was a lavish banquet in Saudi Arabia in honor of the visit by Her Majesty Queen Elizabeth and the Duke of Edinburgh.

All that day refrigerated vans had sped the best of Arab and imported delicacies between Riyadh, the Saudi capital, and a spot in the desert, marked by a mammoth tent. Lobster had been flown in from Jeddah, and truffles from France, and fifty lambs had been slaughtered for the occasion, which was to be attended by hundreds of sheikhs. The hospitable Saudis had even extended the invitation to include the press – an unheard-of event in royal circles – which was how I found myself dining with the Queen, Her Majesty being obscured, however, by pyramids of dates.

Between these two remarkable occasions lie a wealth of memories and a host of meals – of which many are recaptured in *Cooking the Middle Eastern Way.*

The current interest in Middle Eastern cooking is part of a Western trend towards ethnic food. It also coincides with two significant events which, sadly, typify the Middle East in Western minds.

The first is the agonizing civil war in Lebanon which has uprooted many thousands of Lebanese who have fled abroad and taken their cuisine with them. Many have subsequently opened restaurants so that today one can eat Middle Eastern food in almost any large city in the world.

The second event, more protracted, has been the nationalization of the Arab oil industry. Inestimable wealth disbursed by generous rulers now enables even the poorest Bedouin to enjoy a vacation abroad. The first tourists brought cooks to prepare meals according to Muslim dietary laws, and it was not long before leading hotels in London and Paris were employing Muslim chefs, exposing Westerners to Middle Eastern cuisine.

The taste for Middle Eastern food reached the United States with business travelers and tour groups returning from trips. Expatriates employed in places such as Iraq and Iran also enthused about ethnic cooking.

In consequence there is an enormous curiosity about Middle Eastern cooking, but most restaurants serve only a limited number of dishes. This does not mean that *Cooking the Middle Eastern Way* will unveil a thousand and one recipes; what it will do is pass on a few of the most popular so that anyone with a moderate knowledge of cooking can make them.

Other recipes are missing for obvious reasons. It is not feasible to try smoking Iraqi *mashgouf* around a fire in your apartment. Nor to cook *khouzi,* an Arab recipe requiring a whole sheep. Without help, sweetmeats such as *knaffeh* and Turkish delight are very time-consuming to prepare. Today's Middle Eastern housewife usually buys them ready-made.

Bread is also frequently purchased from the baker who makes several batches throughout the day. Many breads are too big to bake in a domestic oven and are cooked in a large, beehive-shaped oven or *tanour.* Similar types are sold by Lebanese and Turkish stores or failing this, the Greek *pita* and Indian *naan* are similar. On a recent visit to Sydney I discovered *khoubz* in a supermarket.

An Australian, I was brought up on beef, but since leaving Sydney in 1963, I have traveled extensively in the Muslim world. By now I have visited every country in the Middle East – and North Africa for good measure.

My interest in local food developed after an initial visit to Beirut, the focus of Middle Eastern cookery. Like any Western visitor, I was eager to acquire some recipes in order to entertain at home. I did not want anything too elaborate, since like most working women, cooking time is limited to weekends, but I sought some easily prepared dishes for entertaining on busy week nights.

I trust the same applies to you and that *Cooking the Middle Eastern Way* will bring new pleasures to your table. *Bismillah!*★

CHRISTINE OSBORNE, 1985

★*Bismillah!* (in the name of God!), as expressed by an Arab before eating.

Left *Pounding coffee beans with a traditional wooden mihbash, Jordan.*

Introduction

edia coverage of the sad events in Lebanon, or the Gulf War, gives the impression that the Middle East is a land of blazing guns, yet the millions of citizens going to work in Cairo or Ankara, or the *felaheen* toiling in the fields, represent a far more accurate picture of daily life.

The belly of the Orient, the Middle East sweeps east from Egypt through the countries of the Fertile Crescent as far as Iran and encompasses the vast land mass of the Arabian peninsula. The majority of people speak Arabic and share a common heritage with colorful regional variations in music, costume and cuisine.

While parts of the Middle East are largely desert, elsewhere is as green as Kentucky, as the name, the Fertile Crescent, implies. Other areas are even subtropical like the beautiful palm-fringed coast of Dhofar, in southern Oman, but between these extremes is the rugged Middle East of Bedouin nomads, a mix of pebble plain and dunes.

According to archaeologists and historians, civilization began sometime in the fifth millennium BC in Mesopotamia.

We know little about the diet of the ancient peoples but it seems likely that they had much the same pulses diet as the *felaheen* of today, and because the region was rich in game, grilled gazelle and wild boar were probably popular.

Ancient civilizations and conquering armies have bequeathed to the Middle East a rich architectural heritage: the remains of giant dams, soaring pyramids, and magical-sounding cities such as Persepolis, Petra and Jerash. In the absence of records, one can only assume that peoples of such building expertise also possessed sophisticated culinary skills.

The expansion of the Greek and Roman empires undoubtedly contributed to the cuisine in the Middle East, and the spread of Islam from Arabia introduced humble but wholesome foods.

Ruling from Baghdad, the Abbasid dynasty (786-902 AD) is known to have been passionately interested in cooking. Many popular present-day recipes have origins in Abbasid kitchens.

The Ottoman Empire, introduced the stuffed vegetable dishes so popular in Middle Eastern cookery. British and French mandates following the First World War also added new ideas, but by now Middle Eastern food had finished marinating and while Western dishes were applauded, basic recipes remained unchanged.

The amalgam of so many cuisines makes Middle Eastern food different and at the same time hard to define. Basically it can be described as wholesome and flavorsome, spicy without being Mexican-hot, and notable for several items in particular: *mezze* or appetizers, stuffed vegetables and meats and rich sweetmeats. It is not merely the food, however, which ranks Middle Eastern cooking – not before time – with the world's greatest cuisines, but its presentation and the surroundings in which it is served.

REGIONAL COOKING
THE LEVANT

While Middle Eastern cooking follows a basic theme, there are regional variations: Levantines eat more grilled meat and yoghurt than, say, the Yemenis; Yemenis, on the other hand, like spicy dishes; Persian recipes dabble in a subtle combination of fruit and meat; curries have crept into the Arab cuisine, etc. There is little difference in etiquette except where contact with the West has influenced customs.

The countries of the eastern Mediterranean littoral, or the Levant – Lebanon, Syria and Jordan – enjoy a similar cuisine; however the same dish may be called by different names, which is rather confusing, in the same way that cooking methods – a pinch of this, or a handful of that – are often vague. Of the three cuisines, Jordanian

Opposite above left *A fine bream in Muscat. The Omanis are great fish-eaters.*

Opposite above right *Sifting pulses in Aswan, Upper Egypt.*

Opposite below left *A Bedouin woman making buttermilk in Dubai.*

Opposite below right *Tomato-seller in East Jerusalem souq or bazaar.*

cooking is more basic, a mix of Bedouin food from the eastern desert and warming dishes from the Western escarpment. Syrian cooking tends to be more elaborate, while the best known, Lebanese, is noted for the stylish presentation of food and the infinite variety of dishes.

The flavors of Lebanon are those most commonly associated with Middle Eastern cookery: the tangy taste of chopped mint, garlic and lemon juice in an olive oil dressing; the smoky taste of purées made from roasted sesame seeds and grilled eggplants; the subtle taste of rose water in desserts. While the aroma of Turkish coffee percolates the entire Middle East, this too, is unmistakably Lebanese.

If any race lives to eat, it is the affable Lebanese, a shrewd businessman who finds any excuse is a good reason to mix business with the pleasure of eating.

The Arabic, *lebnan,* is derived from an Aramaic word meaning white, a reference to the snow-covered mountains behind Beirut but also to *laban* which in Lebanon, means curdled milk, a dish of thick, creamy yoghurt being a popular mezze.

Mezze or appetizers are the best known aspect of Lebanese cuisine. They consist of many small dishes, either true *hors d'oeuvre* or miniature main courses, laid out for people to serve themselves as in a Scandinavian *smörgasbord.* Some of the endless *mezze* recipes are described in the first chapter.

A typical meal may consist solely of *mezze* or have several courses such as stuffed meat and vegetable dishes, *kebabs,* a fish or poultry dish, salads and rice, ending with fresh fruit, sweetmeats and coffee. A water pipe, or *nargila,* may be brought in for the men, its gentle bubbling adding to the convivial atmosphere.

Arak is commonly drunk with a *mezze.* Lebanon also produces wines. The Lebanese particularly like eating out of doors, it being debatable whether they, or the Turks, invented the custom of *al fresco* dining.

Syrian food lacks the variety of Lebanese, but it is invariably appetizing. *Mezze* are equally a Syrian tradition. Bulghur is widely used in

Right   *Elaborate silver tamarind juice stand in Damascus, Syria.*

Far right   *A rural baker in Iran. The large loaves of barbari are too big for a domestic oven.*

cooking and Syrian housewives are reputedly the best *kibbeh* makers in the Middle East. Seafood is available on the Mediterranean coast.

Part of the fertile crescent, Syria is self-sufficient in vegetables and fruits – pears, grapes and delicious figs. Preserved apricots are a specialty of Damascus. Together with almonds and walnuts, pistachio nuts are used in the sweetmeats at which Syrian pastrymakers excel. Aleppo is renowned for superb pastries and rich desserts.

Syria produces similar fruity wines to the Lebanon. *Arak* is drunk with *mezze*. Traditional fruit juices – tamarind, orange and pomegranate – are losing ground to bottled soft drinks. Tea is drunk at every opportunity. Coffee is always served with a large glass of water to quench the thirst. Yoghurt-and-water is drunk by the Bedouin.

Several Jordanian dishes have roots in Bedouin cooking.

The best example is *mansaf*, meaning "the large tray" or dish on which this traditional repast is served. A vast communal dinner, it consists of slices of stewed mutton, rice, bread and *jameed* (a dried sheep's milk yoghurt crumbled, melted and poured over the food). Similar to the Arab *khouzi, mansaf* is served on the floor of a tent with everyone sitting around the dish helping himself.

Fatir is a popular people's food, consisting of unleavened bread soaked in yoghurt and topped with *samneh* (or clarified butter).

In Amman *mezze* are popular: variations are *kishki,* or yoghurt mixed with chopped walnuts and olive oil and sprinkled with the lemony spice known as *sumak*. Most *mezze* are an extension of Lebanese cuisine.

Soups are not popular, a reason being the rich sauces which accompany many main courses. Soups made from lentils, meat and vegetables and *frieka* (cracked smoked wheat) are most common, especially in the Western

escarpment overlooking the Dead Sea.

Popular main courses are: *yakneh* (a meat and vegetable casserole), *mahshi* or stuffed vegetables, chicken and *kebabs. Shawarma* (sliced lamb on a skewer) is equally popular in Jordan as it is in Syria or Lebanon.

Like poultry, meat is marinated to tenderize and to absorb flavors. A common custom adds coriander fried with garlic to many recipes: a small wooden pestle and mortar used solely for grinding this mixture is kept in every kitchen. Common vegetables in Jordanian cooking are tomatoes, okra, cabbage and eggplants. Rice is more popular as a side dish than in Syria or Lebanon, a custom linked to basic Bedouin cooking.

Shops in Amman specialize in *knaffeh,* a cream cheese sweetmeat with Palestinian origins. Most local sweetmeats are made throughout the Levant.

Bread is eaten with every meal with many variations on the common, rounded unleavened pocket bread known simply as *khoubz*. People buy *ka'ik bil sim-sim,* a soft bread ring sprinkled with sesame seeds, sold with a boiled egg and a tiny packet of spices, to eat on their way to work.

TURKEY

Ottoman domination of the Middle East had a big influence on ethnic cooking. Many recipes have Turkish origins: who but the Turks would call dishes "Dainty Fingers" or "Lady's Thighs" – *kadın budu?*

The Ottoman sultans' opulent tastes also extended to the kitchen. The largest part of the Topkapı Palace were the kitchens where we are told that some sixty chefs and two hundred assistants devised special delicacies. It is said they had at least forty ways of cooking eggplant and more than sixty ways of making *baklava*. There were specialists for *böreks* (stuffed pastries), cooks for fish, meat and poultry, and makers of sweetmeats.

Based on meat and dairy products,

The subtle use of herbs and spices is a feature of Middle Eastern recipes. Many are native to the region.

Turkish food is high in protein. Plain yoghurt is greatly enjoyed, blended into soups and sauces, or as a flavor in cakes. White cheese is always found in a *meze (mezze)* with other appetizers.

Seafood is popular on the coast while lamb is the basic meat, the *döner kebap* (turning kebab) has traveled to the far corners of the earth with Turkish migrants. *Döner kebap (shawarma* in Arabic) slowly turning on a skewer is a familiar sight. Pieces of lamb are loaded onto a vertical skewer which slowly turns in front of an electric grill. As they cook, they are sliced off into a tray or, if a customer is waiting, into a pocket of *ekmek (pita* bread) which is filled with salad.

Turkish cooks perform miracles with the most mundane vegetables. Plain by any standards, the cabbage is elevated to regal status by stuffing with rice, raisins and pine nuts. The stuffed eggplant dish *Imam bayıldı* (swooning Imam) has captured the imagination of cooks far beyond the Middle East.

Rice is habitually served with main courses; Turks like long-grain rice cooked so that a little moisture remains.

Desserts are those based on milk, such as *muhallabia,* or rice pudding, and those made from pastry such as *baklava.* The most famous sweetmeat is *lokum,* known all over the world as Turkish

Delight.

Traditional beverages are beer, wine and *rakı* (arak). Made from grapes and aniseed, rakı clouds when water is added giving it the popular name of *Aslan sutu* or "lion's milk." Other drinks are *aryan* (yoghurt and water) and *shira* or grape juice. Turkish coffee is served *şekersiz* (without sugar), *orta şekerli* (medium) or *şerkerli* (plenty of sugar).

EGYPT

The origins of some Egyptian recipes can be traced back to Pharoanic times. It is fascinating to consider that *bamieh* or okra stew and *melokhia* leaf soup were as popular then as they are today but it is a disappointment not to find a grand dish that epitomizes Egyptian cooking.

Most recipes contain elements from the whole range of foods generally thought of as Middle Eastern fare, while the *cous-cous* of North Africa is popular. Occupying armies have also influenced the local repertoire and whether the famous *Umm Ali* pudding is actually British or Egyptian is something of a moot question.

The peasant dish *foul medames* (brown bean casserole) is eaten by three-quarters of the population before work.

While most middle class Egyptian households serve *mezze,* they do not reach the elaborate proportions of the Levant. Eaten dipped in *tahini, falafel* (ground bean patties) are a great favorite.

Poultry is greatly prized. Otherwise famous for nightclubs, Kasr el Nil, the avenue leading to the Pyramids, is equally famous for restaurants specializing in roast pigeon.

The Nile Valley produces wonderful vegetables. Citrus fruits are plentiful, the round green lime having a special place in local cooking. Fruit juices – grape, orange and lemon, tamarind and mango – are popular. Tea is widely drunk.

Popular desserts are *Umm Ali* and *muhallabia,* while an old family cook who used to work for the British is sure to produce a good pudding. *Baklava* and *basbousa* are among many sweetmeats. Groppi's tearoom in Cairo is a popular rendezvous for tea and pastries.

ARAB STATES

Apart from Yemen, the cooking is similar throughout Arabia (Saudi Arabia, Bahrain, Kuwait, Qatar, the United Arab Emirates and the Sultanate of Oman). Prior to the wealth from oil and gas deposits, the Arabs lived on a Bedouin diet of dates, rice, and meat when it was available. The coastal communities also ate fish.

All the Arab states enjoy splendid seafood. While the *souqs* and supermarkets are stocked with everything money can buy, some countries have become self-sufficient in certain foods, thus increasing the scope for cooking. The emirate of Ras al-Khaimah produces milk from cattle living in air-conditioned stalls, while Abu Dhabi grows excellent vegetables.

The large number of Indians and Bangladeshis employed as cooks has resulted in many dishes becoming hotter and spicier. On the coast, people are exposed to new foods in hotels. *Mezze* have become an accepted start to a meal and a Kuwaiti, or a Bahraini, enjoys spaghetti just as much as an Italian.

Basmati rice is eaten exclusively by the Arabs. Dried Indian or Omani limes are ground into a powder which, added to food, imparts an unusual tart flavor.

Popular main courses are braised meat with potatoes, *kebabs,* fish and prawn or chicken curries. *Khouzi* is a famous Arab dish prepared on auspicious occasions such as a tribal wedding, or the inauguration of a new airport. In former times, the recipe called for a whole baby camel to be stuffed with a whole sheep stuffed with whole chickens in turn stuffed with hard-boiled eggs and the rest of the cavity stuffed with rice, nuts, raisins and spices. Today a sheep is similarly stuffed and cooked for several hours in a huge *tanour*. When the flesh is tender the carcass is removed and the stuffing spread on top for people to serve themselves.

Such a feast is served on the floor of the living room, or tent. VIPs sit on either side of the host, who breaks off tasty pieces and passes them around. Despite a rather morbid Western preoccupation with the Arab taste for sheep's eyes, the brains and spleen are considered the choice morsels.

Mineral water, soft drinks or yoghurt drinks are common beverages.

Fruit and dates are served after dinner. Oases near Nizwa, in the rugged interior of Oman, produce some of the best dates in Arabia. *Muhammar*, a sweetened rice, is popular.

Coffee, usually Nescafé, and sweet black tea are served afterwards. *Qahwa*, coffee brewed with cardamom husks, is offered ritually on other occasions.

YEMEN
Traditional Yemeni food is unknown outside Yemen, a wildly beautiful country barely out of the Middle Ages.

Local diet is based on several highly original dishes that can be attributed to the country's long isolation. Others show an Ottoman influence, while a taste for spicy foods results from contact with Indian traders on the Tihama or Red Sea coast.

Food is always fresh. No Yemeni housewife would dream of dishing up leftovers; what is not eaten is distributed among the less fortunate. A negative side is that most dishes are served boiling hot and thus lose their nutritional value. Due to economic restraints, few dishes are very nourishing and the truly unique Yemeni recipes are unlikely to appeal to a Western palate. Others common to Middle Eastern cookery – lentil soup,

okra stew – appear in this book.

Bread is the basis of every meal; the most common is a round, unleavened bread baked from sorghum flour, which is ground by the housewife or taken to the local miller. *Bint al sahin* is a cross between bread and a pudding, eaten hot as a savory dish or smothered with *samneh* and honey.

The consumption of fresh milk is rare. Sheep or goat's milk is soured by prolonged vigorous shaking in a gourd, the resultant buttermilk being used in the preparation of many dishes. Farmers in the Tihama foothills make a first class smoked goat's milk cheese, known as *jubn*, which is sold in Ta'iz, the old capital.

Soups are popular, especially in the cooler highlands. The most common is *helba*, based on ground fenugreek seeds which are whipped to a froth, with meat stock, hot pepper and other seasonings.

Similar to the Levant, dips are a tradition, but in Yemen they are different. *Zahawiq*, the best known, is made from tomatoes and chili to which tiny dried fish are sometimes added. *Foul* is eaten daily. Other pulses are made into stews. *Asid* is a thick gruel-like porridge made from sorghum, boiling water, oil and honey or broth. Mutton is the most common meat, the brain and liver being especially revered.

Most days Yemenis forego breakfast in favor of a large lunch before the *qat*-chewing session. Chewed every afternoon, the leaf depresses the appetite, supper in consequence being late and light. On market day, breakfast is a tradition for farmers who travel long distances. Typical breakfasts are chick peas served with fried liver, *fattah* (a dough made from dates, bananas and butter) and *mattit* (egg, tomatoes, peppers and onions made into a soup mixed with crumbled bread, butter and honey).

Most foods are cooked in vegetable oils. *Alya*, lard obtained from the melted down fatty tail of sheep, is

An elaborate table setting during Eid al-fitr, the holiday following Ramadan, the month of fasting.

popular in rural areas. Cooking facilities remain primitive; most women cook over a fire in the kitchen, or at the entrance to their house. When something special is made, it is a custom to send a portion to a neighbor.

When the meal is ready, everyone sits around the cloth, unless strangers are present, when women eat alone. Traditionally served first, men receive the choicest portions of food (a custom throughout the entire Middle East).

A meal is eaten in a special order. The first course is white radish, which is dipped in *helba*. A salad follows, with *bint al sahin*, soup and hot vegetable dishes such as okra and potatoes. The last course is usually mutton stew, or grilled chicken with rice. This menu is typical of a middle class urban family; most Yemenis eat a lot less.

Special foods are eaten during the fast of Ramadan. Similar to other countries in the Middle East, the fast is broken with dates, grapes and other fruits, followed by a large meal. In the mountains, soups replace gruel, while *muhallabia* is a popular Ramadan dessert.

PERSIA

Persian cooking is very sophisticated, a fact not generally known outside Iran. While the country has an advantage over the Arab states in being largely agricultural, local recipes display real genius in combining many unusual ingredients. A good example is meat and prune casserole. Dried fruit soups are also typically Persian.

Bread is served with every meal, an eating aid rather than a food to enjoy.

Salads and appetizers are essential components of a meal. Lettuce and tomato salad and cucumber salad with raisins and yoghurt are very popular.

Thick yoghurt is the base of many salads or *borani* served as appetizers, or *pish ghaza*. Similar to *mezze*, these may consist of as many as forty small dishes and soups set out as a buffet.

Main courses cover a variety of mutton and chicken dishes, usually roasted or stewed with the addition of herbs and spices. Cooked slowly, the sauces become rich and aromatic; some become so thick that when poured over rice they are a substantial meal.

The most famous Persian dish is *chelo kebab*. The best cuts of lamb are thinly sliced and marinated in onion and lemon juice. After brief cooking on a charcoal fire, they are arranged on a cushion of fluffy rice. Dabs of butter and a raw egg yolk are mixed into the rice and *sumak* is sprinkled on top. Slivers of onion, radishes and sprigs of parsley are served as garnishes. A queue outside a restaurant indicates they serve good *chelo kebab*.

The various ways of cooking rice in Persia have no equal in the Middle East; popular are steamed rice or *chelo* (see page 76) and *katteh*, a molded rice served in wedges.

The Persian caviar fishing industry is centred in Babolsar on the Caspian Sea. The gray-green beluga caviar from the elephant sturgeon is the best quality. Sturgeon themselves are a great delicacy. The thick fillets are lightly smoked and served poached with a green lemon juice dressing. Rural restaurants serve grilled trout, while the Gulf cities enjoy good seafood in common with most Arab countries.

Desserts tend to be either rather heavy or very sweet, a general trend throughout the Middle East. Popular desserts are stuffed apples and quinces.

The country produces an abundance of fruits – oranges, peaches, pomegranates and succulent watermelons from the Isfahan Oasis. Many fruits are made into *sharbats* – from which the word *sorbet* derives.

Extolled by Farsi poets, Persian wine was of considerable quality, one of the main wine growing regions being around Shiraz, "the city of wine and roses." *Abdug* or yoghurt-and-

water is drunk during a meal. People drink tea rather than coffee.

IRAQ

The art of Middle Eastern cookery reached its zenith during the Abbasid era in Baghdad – the city of Sheherezade and "a thousand and one nights."

The culinary skills of Abbasid chefs were renowned: great chefs were presented at court, the lavishness of their creations was extolled by poets, and lengthy treatises were written on the noble art of cookery. Ancient cookery manuals refer to banquets lasting for days, with table after table laden with roast partridges, ducks and francolins that had been marinated overnight in curd, milk-fed kid and spitted gazelle, and platters of sweetmeats.

With the exception of one or two regional dishes, Iraqi cooking follows general trends with a historic Persian bias. While most Iraqis eat sparingly, when they do eat, it resembles a last supper. An Iraqi dining table is invariably loaded with exotic foods.

Appetizers are usually stuffed potatoes, *dolmas* and salads. Spiked with mint, yoghurt is popular, while rice dishes are similar to Persian varieties. The most elaborate, *timman za'fran*, includes ground meat, raisins and nuts – a substantial meal.

A variation on the famous Saudi *khouzi* steams a whole lamb on a domestic stove, then barbecues it over a bed of rice in a *tanour*. Suspended head down, the fatty tail constantly bastes the carcass as it melts.

Parks and gardens line the Tigris River flowing through Baghdad, where restaurants are set out under the trees. A traditional dish is *mashgouf*, a flavorsome fish which is slowly smoked around an open fire and served with sliced tomatoes, onions and bread.

Fish and dates are twin products in Basra, at the head of the Arabian Gulf. Dates have a myriad uses – barbecued

Among themselves, most Arab families eat off a cloth spread on the living-room floor. However, if a Western guest is present, a table will be set with crockery and cutlery.

fish with date purée is typical of Basra, dates are made into *halwa,* a toffee-like sweet, and stuffed in pastries.

Mentioned in the *Arabian Nights,* the sweet, orange colored rosettes known as *zlabiya* are still popular.

Sweetmeats and coffee are served in the living room. If people have used their fingers to eat, a servant may bring a jug of water and soap to wash. Most urban houses have Western-type bathrooms.

ETIQUETTE, CUSTOMS AND COOKING TIPS

Living an isolated existence in the desert, a Bedouin nomad displays the same characteristics as an American family out in the Midwest, or Australians in the outback. Hospitality is second nature: while having no idea from where their next meal may come, they will offer what they have – their last bread or dates. In extending their hospitality, reflected in the coffee ceremony (see pages 142 to 151), they consider it their duty to protect a guest, even a perfect stranger. As more and more Bedouin exchange nomadism for a sedentary life, these same unwritten rules apply in the city.

There are certain rules of etiquette in the Middle East which *Orientales,* as people refer to themselves, have observed since the revelations of the holy *Quran.* "Cleanliness is next to godliness", is a saying that may have come from Muslim society. It is unthinkable not to wash before saying one's prayers, or sitting down to eat. Even basic Arab restaurants have a corner basin. Incense is frequently burned to purify the air.

A strict code of etiquette at mealtimes expresses subtle distinctions among the diners. An important guest will be offered special delicacies such as the tail of the chicken, and so on. The host has the first taste, a custom to show the food is worthy of being eaten and to encourage others to eat.

A meal always commences with thanks to Allah, the provider – *bismillah!* Morsels of food are taken or accepted using only the right hand. One should never refuse pieces offered by one's host as it is considered impolite. If seated on the floor, the soles of one's feet must not be displayed as this, too, is considered ill-mannered. Other aspects of local etiquette are similar to Western table manners: not to fill one's mouth too full, not to finish eating first in order not to embarrass others.

DIETARY LAWS

Muslim dietary laws are prescribed in the *Quran,* the book of revelations of the Angel Gabriel to the Prophet Muhammed in sixth-century Arabia and later transcribed by his companions.

Food is frequently mentioned, the major rules being abstention from eating the flesh of swine, the blood of any animal, or indeed eating any animal that has not been slaughtered in the correct manner by a Muslim (*hilal*). Muslims slit the throat of a beast, at the same time repeating the phrase: "In the name of God, God is most great!" Inebriating liquors are forbidden.

SPICES

Middle Eastern food is characterized by the subtle use of spices bought in the *attarine* or spice street, where traders squat in tiny shops among boxes of colorful spices.

While today the emphasis is on the value of spices as flavorings, they have wide-ranging uses in homeopathic remedies, as vegetable dyes and in purification rituals.

Cassia and cinnamon were essential components in Egyptian embalming oils. Frankincense and cinnamon were among the gifts taken by the Queen of Sheba on her historic journey to Jerusalem. Frankincense and myrrh were also offered to the infant Jesus in Bethlehem.

Contact with the East inevitably introduced spices to Western kitchens;

crusading knights brought new ideas for flavorings; and the use of spices in Abbasid society was second to none.

The following spices are commonly used in Middle Eastern cooking.

A native of the Middle East, anise is cultivated for its small, oil-bearing seeds. Allspice is a fragrant spice, like a blend of cinnamon, nutmeg and cloves, used in stuffings.

The Middle East is the world's biggest importer of cardamom, whose crushed seeds are blended with meat dishes, while the whole pods flavor desserts and coffee.

While paprika, or red pepper is used in many regions, hotter spices such as chili are generally restricted to the Yemen. Cinnamon is used in a variety of dishes, while cloves are used to flavor veal and other delicate dishes. Coriander is another native spice which Mesopotamian records claim was cultivated in the fabled "Hanging Gardens of Babylon."

The "queen of spices", cumin, is also a native of the Middle East. Its delicate aroma complements many vegetable dishes and salads – *falafel* need a good pinch of cumin to enliven their flavor. Used ground, or whole, cumin is an ingredient in Gulf fish curries. Ground fenugreek seeds help thicken curries and are excellent served with potatoes and eggplants.

Ginger figures in many medieval recipes, its medicinal value being noted in the *Quran*. Ginger tea is a soothing beverage. Abbasid society used nutmeg as a remedy for intestinal disorders; today it is used as a flavor and garnish in desserts.

The world's most popular spice, pepper, is used to flavor savory dishes, and if pepper tops the popularity poll, then saffron is the world's most expensive spice. It requires over 250,000 crocus stigmas to make a pound of saffron but only a strand or two to give a beautiful golden glow to rice and poultry dishes. Turmeric, a yellow Indian spice, is a much cheaper substitute.

Sesame seed is an historically valuable spice in the Middle East. Raw or roasted, its seeds flavor many dishes and breads. The oil is used on salads and in cooking.

FESTIVALS

There are several important religious festivals in the Muslim calendar.

Eid al-fitr is observed on the tenth month following Ramadan, the month of fasting, fasting from dawn until dusk being considered good self-discipline and spiritually uplifting.

It begins when the new moon is sighted over Mecca, in Saudi Arabia. Special sweets are made; *nahash*, a cream cheese and filo pastry, is a Syrian specialty made at this time.

COOKING UTENSILS

Being very old, most of the recipes in this book were originally cooked using unsophisticated utensils on primitive stoves. A modern person cooking the Middle Eastern way needs only three or four basic items in addition to normal kitchen utensils: a large, deep skillet, preferably made of cast iron; a pestle and mortar; and a blender or food processor.

COOKING INGREDIENTS

Cooking oils are basically vegetable oils such as corn, sesamé seed, other nut oils, and sunflower oil. Dishes to be eaten cold are made with olive oil, which is the foundation of all dressings.

Samneh is melted butter, clarified by straining the oil through a thin piece of muslin which extracts any impurities and imparts a richer taste. Like *alya, samneh* is mainly used by rural communites.

Other items to have in stock for cooking the Middle Eastern way are *bulghur,* or cracked wheat; *tahina* or *tahini; filo* pastry; flavorings such as orange blossom and rose water; and a supply of almonds, pine nuts, walnuts, and pistachios.

Mezze *(Hors d'oeuvre or Appetizers)*

Beirut used to be an enchanting city. Standing with its feet in the blue Mediterranean and with its back to snowcapped Mount Lebanon, it was cultured, sophisticated and fun-loving. It also had some of the finest restaurants in the Middle East.

I first visited Lebanon in 1970 to write some travel articles. Then in 1977 I returned to photograph war-torn Beirut for *The Times*. It was a brief acquaintance, but one of special significance to my subsequent interest in Middle Eastern cookery.

On this initial visit, with a friend, we chose to eat in a restaurant at Pigeon Grotto, a popular family outing from Beirut. Having ordered *mezze*, we were choosing a main course when the *maître d'hôtel* suggested that *mezze* would probably suffice. Imagine our relief, therefore, when plate after plate of appetizers was brought to the table. Counted, they numbered twenty-five and were obviously a substantial meal.

Essentially a Lebanese creation, *mezze* assume the aura of a banquet when prepared by a cook of repute. A way of life in Lebanon, Syria and Turkey, *mezze* have been adopted by other countries in the Middle East. As many as seventy dishes may be served in a large *mezze* on an auspicious occasion such as a marriage.

Making a pocket-bread sandwich in a Cairo snackbar.

Next page   Mezze or appetizers. A large mezze table may have up to 70 small dishes.

Items may be miniatures of a main course or true *hors d'oeuvre*, similar to a Scandinavian *smörgasbord*. Their preparation is time-consuming, but many *mezze* can be made beforehand and chilled. Others such as sautéed fries should be served fresh for best results. Ideally you need someone to help, either to cook or to run the dishes out.

You can plan *mezze* around whatever you like, but there are about a dozen basic items without which even a small *mezze* is incomplete. First, the *mezze* table must always have a basket of freshly made bread, the round, unleavened bread known vaguely as *khoubz Arabieh*, is used instead of cutlery to pick up morsels of food. It is also essential for the dips.

Three or four dips are always found on a *mezze* table. The best known is *hummus*, a creamy corn-colored paste made from mashed chick peas and *tahini*, a paste made from sesame seed meal blended with lemon juice and spices. Another popular dip is *babagannouj*, a pleasant, smoky-tasting dip made from grilled, mashed eggplant, garlic and *tahini*. I love it, one dish of *babagannouj* never being enough as I sit talking, dipping bread in it.

Taramasalata is a flesh-colored purée made from fish roe. Bread and celery sticks are dipped in *taramasalata* which *must* be home-made. Made from strained yoghurt, thick, creamy *labneh* is always part of a *mezze*. In contrast, a purée of red pepper and walnuts, *muhammara*, is a hot dip. Both keep well in the refrigerator.

Another familiar constituent of *mezze* is stuffed vine leaves. These are popular throughout the Middle East, either hot with a ground meat filling, or cold with rice and pine nuts.

Lebanese cooking suffers only one handicap in that there is no good beef available, true throughout the Middle East, which is not cattle country. Since mutton is also frequently poor quality, this is chiefly why so many seasonings are used and why meat is so often ground and eaten as chopped meat. Usually there are at least two types of ground meat dishes in a basic *mezze*. *Kibbeh nayé* consists of raw, seasoned ground lamb. This mixture can be combined with other ingredients, made into meatballs, and fried.

Strips of fried liver and *sanbusak* or *börek* (pastries) filled with ground meat, cream cheese and spinach, are also popular *mezze*. Artichoke hearts, brains (both with lemon and olive oil dressing), cubes of white cheese, celery, olives and pickled sweet peppers are easy-to-serve cold dishes. And one could go on endlessly listing more dishes – *falafel* (mashed *lima* bean or chick pea patties), fried mussels, chicken wings grilled with garlic and yoghurt sauce, miniature pizzas . . .

But, finally, there is *tabbouleh*, or the Lebanese national salad, without which no *mezze* is complete. Very refreshing, it has a crunchy texture from the cracked wheat and a tangy taste from the lemon. It must be served fresh.

By tradition, *mezze* are eaten with *arak* (*rakı* in Turkey), a spirit similar to *pastis* drinks such as Pernod.

Babagannouj *Eggplant Dip*

Serves about 4:

2 large eggplants
¼ cup plus 2 tablespoons tahini (sesame seed paste)
juice of 2 lemons
2 cloves garlic, crushed
¼ tablespoons salt
pepper to taste
1 tablespoon finely chopped parsley
olive oil

Slit the skin of the eggplants – this will allow the steam to escape during cooking – then bake or broil gently until the outside is charred and crisp and it begins to split. Scoop out the pulp and mash thoroughly.

Mix this with the *tahini*, lemon juice, garlic, salt and pepper and continue blending to a smooth consistency. If the mixture seems too thick, add some water – which will turn it a whiter color.

Serve in a glass or pottery dish garnished with the chopped parsley and, finally, pour a teaspoon of olive oil into the center.

Babagannouj is most often eaten as a dip with Arab bread, but it can also be served as a salad with black olives and tomato slices.

Babagannouj is a smoky dip made from grilled eggplants.

Hummus *Chick Pea Dip*

Serves about 6:
2¼ cups whole chick peas
1 teaspoon bicarbonate of soda
1-2 cloves garlic, crushed
salt
¼ cup plus 2 tablespoons
  tahini (sesame seed paste)
1½-2 lemons
4 tablespoons olive oil
a pinch of paprika
finely chopped parsley

Soak the chick peas in plenty of cold water overnight. Drain, add the bicarbonate of soda and cover with water. In a pressure-cooker, steam for about 20 minutes, or simmer for 1½ hours in a pan. Drain the chick peas, reserving the liquid, then set aside a few peas for garnish.

Using a little of the cooking liquid, reduce the rest of the chick peas to a purée in a blender or processor. Add the garlic, salt and *tahini*, and blend together thoroughly. Lastly pour in the lemon juice,

by which time the *hummus* should have a rich, creamy consistency.

Pour into a shallow, concave dish (about the size of a salad plate), pour the oil in the center, and garnish with the whole chick peas. Sprinkle the paprika and a little chopped parsley as a decoration around the edges.

Hummus should be served at room temperature as a dip with warmed Arab bread. It also makes a tasty accompaniment to grilled kebabs.

Taramasalata *Fish Roe Dip*

Serves about 4:
4 thick slices stale white bread
¼ cup plus 2 tablespoons cold
  milk
½ cup fish roe (see method)
1 clove garlic, crushed
½ small onion, finely minced
juice of 1-2 lemons, to taste
1 egg yolk
¼ cup plus 2 tablespoons
  olive oil

The most authentic roe to use is *tarama*, the dried and salted roe of the grey mullet. Smoked cod's roe can be used instead, in which case the skins will need to be removed first.

Remove the crusts and soak the bread in the cold milk. Meanwhile, beat the roe thoroughly in a mortar or in a blender until it is soft.

Squeeze the bread dry and crumble into the roe. Add the garlic and onion, half the lemon juice and beat (or blend) to a creamy paste. When it is smooth, break in the egg

yolk and continue to beat or blend while dribbling in the olive oil and the rest of the lemon juice.

Chill and serve as a dip with whole radishes, black olives, celery stalks, and Arab bread.

Most taramasalata sold commercially is artificially colored and tastes nothing like the home-made version. It keeps for about 10 days in a sealed container in the refrigerator.

Tahini *Sesame Paste Dip*

Serves about 4:
2 cloves garlic, crushed
salt to taste
juice of 2 large lemons
½ cup tahini (sesame seed
  paste)
pinch of ground cumin
1 tablespoon finely chopped
  parsley

Crush the garlic and salt together. Mix with a little lemon juice and blend with the *tahini*. Add the cumin and remaining lemon juice to form a smooth paste, like peanut butter.

Use more garlic if you want the *tahini* to taste stronger. If it is too thick, reduce it with water. As with *hummus*, a blender is ideal for making *tahini*: the result will be smoother and creamier than if made by hand.

Serve in a bowl, and garnish with the parsley.

Mezze dips made from chick peas, fish roe and sesame seed paste. Hummus (left), taramasalata (center) and tahini (below).

Dolma *Stuffed Vine Leaves*

Stuffed vine leaves are popular in the eastern Mediterranean countries.

Serves about 10:
50 vine leaves
1 large onion, finely chopped
3 tablespoons olive oil
1 lb lean lamb or beef, finely ground
½ cup short-grain rice
¼ cup fresh mint, chopped (or 2 teaspoons dried)
¼ cup fresh dill weed, chopped (or 2 teaspoons dried)
salt and freshly ground black pepper
¼ cup plus 2 tablespoons broth
juice of 1-2 lemons
1 lemon, sliced thinly

Cut the stems off the leaves and place them in a large bowl. Pour boiling water over them, and leave to soak for about 20 minutes – this makes them pliable. Drain and cool.

Sauté the onion in the oil until it is soft. Add the meat and cook until it changes color. Add the rice, herbs and salt and pepper, stirring gently over a low heat until the rice is coated and glazed with the oil.

Add the broth and simmer on a medium heat until the liquid is absorbed. Finally mix in the lemon juice. Set aside and allow to cool.

Line the base of a heavy pan with two or three of the vine leaves. Lay the remainder, shiny side down, on a wooden surface and place a teaspoon of the meat mixture in the center.

Roll up each leaf with the sides neatly tucked in, and stack in layers in the pan. Place slices of lemon between each layer. Place a heatproof dish on top of the leaves to hold them down, pour in water almost to the top, cover with a lid and cook for 30 minutes, or until the rice is tender. The vine leaves should be slightly chewy.

Serve lukewarm, sprinkled with some more lemon juice.

Labneh *Thick Yoghurt*

Serves about 4:
2 cups plain yoghurt
salt to taste
finely chopped fresh mint, to
    garnish
olive oil

Fold a large piece of damp cheesecloth in half, and place over a large bowl. Pour the yoghurt into the center of the cloth, tie the cloth corners together with string and suspend over the top of the bowl overnight.

Remove from the cloth, tip into a bowl, stir in the salt and chill. Garnish with chopped fresh mint and a trickle of olive oil in the center.

Labneh will keep a week in a sealed container in the refrigerator. Serve with Arab bread as a dip. In many Middle Eastern countries it is eaten with olives for breakfast.

Labneh is a wholesome
yoghurt dip.
Muhammara (above) *is a hot*
dip excellent with grilled
meats.

Muhammara *Hot Pepper Dip* (picture on page 27)

Serves about 6:

3 medium onions, finely
   chopped
½ cup plus 1 tablespoon olive
   oil
¾ cup crushed walnuts
¾ cup breadcrumbs blended
   with cold water to a purée
2 tablespoons paprika (or 1
   teaspoon chili powder for a
   very hot muhammara) or
   1 small can hot pepper
   purée
a pinch of ground cumin
salt
1 tablespoon pine nuts sautéed
   in a little oil

Using a deep skillet, sauté the onions
gently in the oil until soft and golden. Add
the walnuts, the breadcrumb purée, the
pepper (chili or purée), the cumin and salt
to taste. Continue to sauté gently on a low
heat until the ingredients are well blended
– about 12 minutes.

Remove from the heat, place in a bowl
and garnish with the pine nuts.

Muhammara is eaten as a dip with bread.
It can also be used as a spicy dip with
kebabs, grilled meats and fish. The
Lebanese also eat it as a spread on toast.

Falafel *Lima Bean Patties*

Serves about 6:

2 cups lima beans
6 scallions, finely chopped
3 cloves garlic, crushed
¾ cup finely chopped parsley
1 teaspoon ground cumin
1 teaspoon ground coriander
¼ teaspoon baking soda
salt and cayenne pepper
oil for deep frying
lemon wedges, to garnish

Soak the beans overnight in plenty of cold
water. The next day, drain and then skin
them. Dry and grind in a food processor, or
pound in a mortar.

Add all the other ingredients (except for
the oil) and blend or pound until it has a
smooth paste-like consistency. Stand
uncovered for 15 minutes, then chill. The
paste will dry out in the refrigerator and the
falafel will be easier to handle.

With moistened hands, take small
lumps, flatten slightly to form a patty
shape and place on a tray. Prepare the
remaining bean mixture in this manner.

Heat a ½ inch oil in a deep heavy pan or
skillet and fry the patties, turning
frequently until they are golden brown.
Drain on kitchen paper and serve garnished
with lemon wedges. *Falafel* are eaten with a
side dish of *tahini* dip.

Right   *Falafel or crunchy
fried bean patties. A popular
Egyptian snack, they are
eaten dipped in tahini.*

Tabbouleh *Lebanese "National" Salad*

Serves 6:
¾ cup fine bulghur (cracked wheat)
¾ cup finely chopped onion
¼ cup plus 2 tablespoons chopped fresh mint
1 cup chopped parsley
2 medium tomatoes, diced
1 cup diced cucumber
salt and pepper to taste
¼ cup olive oil, or more
¼ cup lemon juice, or more
black olives, to garnish

Soak the *bulghur* for 1 hour before preparing the salad. Drain it and squeeze out the moisture. Further dry on a cloth.

Place it in a bowl with the finely chopped onion, and mix together, making sure the onion juice penetrates the grains thoroughly. Add the mint, parsley, tomato, cucumber, seasonings, oil and lemon juice, and mix well. Above all, *tabbouleh* should have a distinctive lemony flavor.

Serve the salad chilled, in a glass dish, decorated with a few black olives. *Tabbouleh* is eaten scooped up in bread or, more traditionally in fresh lettuce leaves.

Artichoke Hearts In Olive Oil

Serves 4:
6 small fresh artichokes
½ cup lemon juice
2 cloves garlic, halved
½ cup olive oil
salt and pepper

Remove the stalk and outer leaves and drop the hearts into a bowl of cold water acidulated with a few drops of the lemon juice.

Place the hearts in a heavy pan with 1½ cups water, half the quantities of lemon juice and olive oil and the garlic. Season with salt and pepper, then bring to the boil. Simmer uncovered until the hearts are tender, about 20–30 minutes.

Remove the hearts from the liquid and cool. Mix the rest of the oil and lemon juice with half the remaining liquid, add more seasoning to taste, and cover the hearts with this. Serve cold.

Sanbusak *Stuffed Crescent Pastries*

Makes about 20 sanbusaks:
Pastry
½ stick butter
¼ cup oil
¼ cup water
1 teaspoon salt
1 cup all-purpose flour
egg yolk, or milk to glaze

Sanbusak (or börek in Turkish) are savory pastries stuffed with meat, spinach or cheese. Serve hot or cold.

To make the pastry, melt the butter gently and pour into a china bowl. Add the oil, water and salt and stir well.

Add the flour, a tablespoonful at a time, mixing in thoroughly. Any lumps will gradually disappear. The consistency is correct when pieces of pastry flake off the sides of the bowl, and you can form a ball of smooth dough in your hands.

While you are stuffing the *sanbusaks*, preheat the oven to 375°F.

To make a *sanbusak*, break off a walnut-sized piece of pastry, and roll to a circle of about 3 inches in diameter. Put a teaspoon of the filling on one-half of the circle, taking care not to over-fill (the mixture expands during the cooking), and fold the other half over the filling.

Close the sides of the pastry well by crimping with your finger and thumb. Continue until pastry and filling are used up.

Lay each *sanbusak* side by side in a baking dish, glaze with egg yolk or milk, and bake until golden brown – about 30 minutes.

Cheese Filling

8 oz white cheese (Greek Feta
  is ideal)
pepper
2 hard boiled eggs, diced
½ cup chopped parsley or
  chives

Mix the ingredients to a paste and stuff the
sanbusak as described. It is not necessary to
use salt with a salty white cheese.

Meat Filling

1 medium onion, finely
  chopped
½ cup pine nuts
2 tablespoons butter
½ lb lean lamb or beef, finely
  ground
½ teaspoon allspice
salt and pepper to taste

Sauté the onion and nuts in the butter until
golden. Add the meat, salt and allspice, and
cook gently until the meat changes color,
about 12-15 minutes. Remove from the
pan and cool. Use to stuff the *sanbusak* as
described.

Spinach Filling

2 cups cooked spinach
1 medium onion, finely
  chopped
olive oil
½ cup crumbled white cheese
salt and white pepper
a pinch of paprika

Remove and discard stems, large veins etc.
from the spinach, then wash, drain and
chop the leaves finely.
   Sauté the onion in a little oil until soft and
golden. Add the spinach and seasonings
and cook until tender. Allow to cool, then
mix in the cheese before stuffing the
sanbusaks as described.

Kadın Budu *"Lady's Thighs"*

Serves about 4:
*1 lb lean beef or lamb, finely
    ground*
2 eggs
¼ cup rice
1 teaspoon oil
*1 medium onion, finely
    chopped*
*3 tablespoons finely chopped
    parsley*
salt and pepper
1 stick butter

Knead the meat well in a large bowl, then add one of the eggs, the rice, oil, chopped onion and parsley. Season and mix very well with the meat to form a smooth paste.

With moistened hands, break off lumps and shape into walnut-sized balls. Place in a skillet with a cup of water and simmer gently for 30 minutes. Drain and cool.

Beat the remaining egg, dip the meat balls in it, then roll them in flour. Cook in the melted butter on a high heat until they are crisp and brown. Keep warm until ready to serve.

Kibbeh Nayé *Raw Seasoned Meat with bulghur*

Serves about 4:
*½ cup bulghur or cracked
   wheat
2 medium onions, very finely
   ground
1 lb top quality beef, ground
a generous pinch of paprika
salt and freshly ground black
   pepper, to taste*

Wash and soak the *bulghur* in cold water, about 2 hours. Squeeze dry in cheesecloth.

Grate the onion in a food processor, add the meat, bulghur and seasonings, and mix to a paste–like consistency.

Take small portions of the *kibbeh* mixture and roll into finger shapes in the palms of your hands. Place on a bed of lettuce leaves and splash with olive oil and lemon juice. Garnish with cayenne pepper, as desired.

Kibbeh nayé is the Middle Eastern version of *steak tartare*. To spice it up, you may care to add more Western-style ingredients such as a splash of Worcestershire sauce, Tabasco etc. Other ways of serving it include flattening the mixture in a glass dish. Serve with a dish of lettuce leaves to scoop up small portions.

Brains in Lemon and Olive Oil Dressing

Serves 6:
4 sets lamb's brains
salt and white pepper, to taste
1/3 cup vinegar
1/2 lemon, sliced
1/2 onion, sliced
juice of 1 1/2-2 lemons
1/4 cup plus 2 tablespoons
  olive oil
3 tablespoons finely chopped
  parsley
1/2 clove garlic, crushed

Under a cold tap, remove the brain membranes and clean thoroughly. Put the brains in a pan, add 4 cups of water, the vinegar, lemon and onion slices, and a pinch of salt. Cover and simmer for 15 minutes on a low heat. Do not cook too vigorously or the brains will break. Leave to cool, then drain.

Now cut the brains into quarters. Blend the lemon juice, oil, parsley, garlic and seasonings to taste and cover with this sauce. Serve chilled with a lemon wedge and garnish of parsley.

Fried Liver

Serves about 4:
1/2 lb lamb's or calf's liver
salt and pepper
1 clove garlic, crushed
a pinch of paprika
2 tablespoons butter
1/4 cup lemon juice
parsley, to garnish

Soak the liver for 30 minutes in cold, salted water. Remove, pat dry on kitchen paper and cut the slices into thin strips.

Rub the salt, pepper and garlic into the liver strips, then sprinkle with paprika.

Heat the butter, add lemon juice and toss the liver in it over a high heat for about 1/2 minute each side. Remove to a dish and serve immediately, garnished with the parsley.

Beid Ghanam *Sautéed Lamb's Fries*

Serves about 4:
about 1/2 lb lamb's fries
salt
vinegar
lemon and onion slices
1 clove garlic, crushed
1 stick butter
1/4 teaspoon mixed herbs
white pepper
juice of 1 lemon
finely chopped parsley, to
  garnish

To clean the fries, first remove the outer skin by slicing the sac and pushing the fries out. Separate the sac by cutting the connected duct. Discard the sac and rinse the fries under cold running water. Parboil the fries in salted water (1 tablespoon to 1 pint of water) for five minutes. Drain, cool, remove any veins and cut into small cubes.

Sauté the crushed garlic in melted butter, then add the herbs, salt and pepper. Toss the fries lightly in the butter until golden brown. Do not overcook. Finally add the lemon juice and serve hot, garnished with finely chopped parsley.

Chicken Wings with Garlic and Yoghurt

Serves about 4:
8 chicken wings, cut in half
1/2 cup lemon juice
2 cloves garlic, crushed
1 teaspoon paprika
salt and white pepper
3/4 cup plain yoghurt
parsley, to garnish

Marinate the wings in lemon juice with crushed garlic and seasonings for 1 hour, turning occasionally. Remove and drain.

Mix the yoghurt into the marinade, then brush onto the wings. Broil under a medium heat. As the yoghurt dries, brush more on. The wings should become brown and crisp. Serve warm, garnished with parsley.

Chicken wings spiked with garlic and lemon can be served hot or cold.

Fried Mussels

Serves 8-10:
40 large mussels, scrubbed and cleaned
oil for deep frying
flour for coating
lemon wedges and parsley, to garnish

White sauce
4 tablespoons butter
1/3 cup flour
1 cup milk
a good pinch of mace
salt and pepper

Batter
1 package active dry yeast
a pinch of sugar
2 tablespoons oil
salt
1 cup all-purpose flour, sifted
1/2 cup water, or enough to make the consistency of light cream

Tarator sauce
2 slices stale white bread, soaked in water and squeezed dry
1/2 cup ground almonds or pine nuts
2 cloves garlic, crushed
juice of 1 lemon
1/2 cup olive oil, or more
salt and pepper to taste

Make the white sauce and the batter first, and allow to stand while you prepare the mussels. For the white sauce, melt the butter in a pan, stir in the flour, and then add the milk gradually, stirring all the time. Add the seasonings, and simmer gently until thick. Cover with a butter wrapper and leave to cool. For the batter, dissolve the yeast in a little water with the sugar, and leave to froth, about 10 minutes. Mix the yeast, oil and salt into the flour, and add enough water to give the consistency of half and half.

Wash the mussels under running water, using a brush and knife to remove whiskers and any barnacles. Discard any that are open. Make sure any sand or grit is thoroughly rinsed off.

Boil the mussels vigorously in salted water until the shells open, about 5 minutes. Discard any that have not opened. Allow to cool, then remove each mussel from its shell and place on a board. Retain the mussel stock.

Heat the oil in a deep pan. Coat each mussel with white sauce, then dip it in the flour and then the batter. Drop into the sizzling oil, and deep-fry until crisp and golden, about 1 minute on a high heat.

Drain and serve immediately on a plate garnished with fresh parsley and lemon wedges. Mix the *tarator* sauce ingredients together in a blender, adding enough oil to make a creamy paste.

In the West mayonnaise or tartare sauce might be served with these fried mussels. In most Middle Eastern countries, however, *tarator* sauce is very popular. Spear the mussels with toothpicks and dip them into the sauce.

Mussels fried in batter are common mezze in Lebanon and Turkey. Dried fish sticks are also popular.

Pickled Sweet Peppers

1 lb small sweet peppers
1 small dried chili
2 tablespoons salt
1¼ cup water
½ cup white vinegar

Prick the peppers all over so that they will absorb the marinade. Pack tightly together in a large glass jar with the chili. Add salt, water and vinegar, ensuring that there is no air trapped between the peppers.

Seal and store for three weeks by which time the peppers will be soft and flavorful. Remove the amount required, drain and serve.

Khoubz Arabieh *Arab Bread*

Makes about 20 portions:
2½ cups warm water
1 package active dry yeast
1 tablespoon salt
6 cups wholewheat flour
2 tablespoons corn or other
*   vegetable oil*

No mezze section would be complete without a basic recipe for flat bread.

A cool, crisp accompaniment to Arab bread – salty Feta Cheese, black olives and fingers of celery.

Pour the water into a large mixing bowl and sprinkle yeast on the surface. Add the salt and stir until both are dissolved. Gradually add the flour and knead until you have a soft, pliable dough. Add more flour or water as necessary.

Turn the dough ball into a greased bowl, cover with a cloth and allow to rise, about 2 hours. When doubled in size, punch down and divide into 20 equal portions, and roll into ball shapes. Place each ball on a floured work board, dust with more flour, cover with a cloth and allow to stand a further 15 minutes.

Next roll each ball flat, about 6 inches in diameter, and place on a greased baking sheet in a preheated oven about 375°F. Bake about 15 minutes until slightly brown and puffy. Serve warm. The pockets can be used for stuffing as in *shawarma*.

Soups

On one of my frequent visits to Jordan, my driver took the twisting King's Highway en route to Petra, via Kerak, a town in the Western escarpment. It was late March and from being a sunny day, the weather suddenly turned black, lightning crackled over the Dead Sea and wind drove sheets of hail against our windscreen. Adeb and I had intended stopping only for a coffee in Kerak, a town known for its lofty, Crusader-built castle, but instead we lingered over a warming bowl of soup. Feast-day Soup is a traditional dish, especially among Jordan's minority Christian community, of whom many live in this area and around Madaba. Dipping in chunks of bread, we found it sustained us for the rest of our journey.

While soups tend to be uncommon in the hot, desert states, they are widely cooked in countries such as Turkey, Syria and Iraq with colder climates. Old Middle Eastern recipe manuals show an infinite number of meat and vegetable soups and many different combinations of both.

Lentil is the most popular, especially in Egypt where *felaheen* may eat it three times a day. The dried pulses that are so widely cultivated in Egypt, Iraq and the Levant – lentils, broad beans, chick peas, split peas and others – make thick, creamy soups or *shorbah* (in Arabic).

Other soups such as vegetable soup are so rich in ingredients that they are almost a stew and, eaten with bread, become a meal in themselves. Common vegetable soups are zucchini, carrot and a variety of spinach soups. All use fresh ingredients.

Although I have not given the recipes here, two unusual soups from Egypt and Yemen are *melokhia* and *helba*. Made with a game base and fresh *melokhia* leaves (of the mallow family and resembling mint), the first from ancient Egypt is still prepared almost daily by country women, the proportions varying according to the standard of living. *Helba* is a fiery soup served scalding in earthenware bowls. It is eaten daily throughout North Yemen.

Yoghurt soups are a major soup category, the addition of yoghurt or *laban* adding a wholesome taste to any food. Often the yoghurt is only added at the end, merely stirred in and gently heated (as, if boiled, it will curdle). I once enjoyed a splendid yoghurt soup in a small hotel in Konya, the town of whirling dervishes in central Anatolia. The Turks also use prodigious amounts of yoghurt in their cooking; chilled cucumber and yoghurt soup is a perfect start to a lunch on a hot summer's day.

Many people will already know *avgolemono* from a Greek restaurant. The same soup, egg and lemon, or *beid bi limoun* in Arabic, is common in Turkey and Lebanon. A very nourishing soup, especially for anyone who is convalescing, the recipe here is only one of many delicate versions.

Fish soups are popular along the coasts of Turkey, Syria and Lebanon. The recipe included here comes from Izmir, the Turkish port known for its annual September Trade Fair. Beach restaurants in ill-fated Beirut used to serve wonderful *shorbat al samak* made with fresh Mediterranean fish.

The typical sweet and sour marriage of many sophisticated Persian dishes is found in pomegranate soup, an exotic, if time consuming, dish to make. Both Iranians and Iraqis are particularly fond of zucchini soup, for which there is a simple recipe that gives wonderful results.

A Western touch with many of these soups might be to garnish them with fried croûtons.

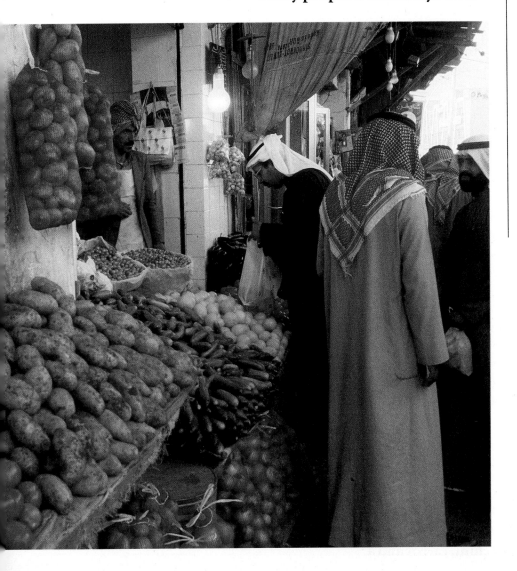

It is the custom for men to shop in Kuwait. The souq is crowded on Thursday morning before Friday, the Muslim holy day.

Egg and Lemon Soup

Serves 6:

5 cups chicken broth, strained
salt and pepper to taste
¼ cup rice
2 eggs
juice of 1 medium lemon
parsley, to garnish

Heat, but do not boil the chicken broth, then season with salt and pepper. Add the rice and cook slowly until tender, about 10–15 minutes.

Meanwhile, prepare the sauce. Beat the eggs in a small bowl, all the while slowly adding the lemon juice.

When ready to serve, slowly add the lemon juice mixture to the soup, warm to almost boiling (the eggs will curdle if it does boil), then stand briefly on the side of the stove. Serve garnished with fresh parsley.

Fish Soup

Serves 6:
2lbs white fish
2 medium onions, chopped
¼ cup plus 2 tablespoons
*   olive oil*
1 small crab, and a handful of
*   mussels*
2 cloves garlic, crushed
1 leek, white part only,
*   chopped*
1 tablespoon cider vinegar
1 teaspoon turmeric
½ teaspoon ground allspice
salt and freshly ground black
*   pepper, to taste*
1 sprig each of fennel and
*   savory*
2 bay leaves
2 egg yolks
juice of 1 lemon
¼ cup finely chopped parsley

Only fresh fish will do for this soup. First sauté the onions in a little of the olive oil. Transfer this to a deep saucepan and add everything except the egg yolks, lemon juice and parsley. Add a good 6 cups of water and simmer for 1½ hours until a rich broth is obtained.

Strain this broth to get a clear soup, or carefully remove any bones, skin and crab-shell. Some cooks put the fish in a cloth and suspend it over a bowl. The juice is allowed to flow through, and then the cloth is wrung out to extract every drop of flavorsome liquid.

Now beat the egg yolks and slowly add the lemon juice. Take a ladle of the broth and add to this mixture, stirring gently. Finally add the egg and lemon mixture to the saucepan of broth, stir well and simmer on a low heat until ready to serve.

Garnish with the parsley and grate more black pepper over the top.

Opposite left *Beid bi limoun or egg and lemon soup.*

A rich fish soup can be made with just about anything you like.

Chilled Cucumber and Yoghurt Soup

Serves 4:
1 large cucumber
2½ cups plain yoghurt
½ cup fresh tomato purée
1 clove garlic, finely chopped
salt to taste
a pinch of ground coriander,
mint and paprika, to garnish

Wipe the cucumber clean, but do not peel it. Chop coarsely, sprinkle with salt and allow to stand for 30 minutes. Rinse and drain, and put it in a blender with the remaining ingredients (except for the paprika). Blend until the soup is creamy. Chill.

Serve in chilled bowls, each garnished with a sprinkling of the paprika.

Carrot Soup

Serves 6:
2 lbs carrots, scraped and sliced
   thinly
½ stick butter
salt and pepper
1 teaspoon sugar
5 cups chicken broth, strained
¼ cup all-purpose flour
1 cup milk
2 egg yolks
finely chopped parsley, to
   garnish

Sauté the carrots in half the butter, then add enough water to cover. Season with the salt and pepper, add the sugar and simmer gently until the carrots are soft. Allow to cool, then put through a blender with the liquid. Now combine the carrot purée and the broth and simmer on a low heat until the purée dissolves into the stock.

Melt the remaining butter in a small pot, add the flour and stir in the milk. When this mixture thickens, take it off the stove and add the egg yolks, beating well.

Add this mixture to the basic soup, mix well and return to the stove. Simmer on a low heat – the yolks will curdle if it boils – then serve, garnished with parsley.

Yoghurt Soup

Serves 4:
1 medium onion, finely
   chopped
½ stick butter
2 cups chicken broth, strained
¼ cup pearl barley, soaked
   overnight
salt and pepper
¼ cup finely chopped parsley
¼ cup dried mint, crushed
1 egg
2 cups plain yoghurt

Sauté the onion in the butter until soft and golden. Add the chicken broth and simmer until just below the boiling point. Add the drained barley and cook until tender – about 20 minutes – then add seasoning and parsley.

Beat the egg lightly, add it to the yoghurt and blend together well. Then add a little warm broth to the yoghurt and mix. Pour the yoghurt slowly into the broth, and stir over a low heat – do not boil, or the yoghurt will curdle – for about 10–15 minutes. A few drops of fresh lemon juice add zest to this delicious soup. Garnish with the mint.

Above left   Chilled cucumber soup is ideal for a summer's day.

Above right   Cheap and easy to make, carrot soup.

Below   The recipe for yoghurt soup has Armenian origins.

Feast-day Soup

Serves about 4:
1 lb lean lamb, finely ground
salt and freshly ground black
    pepper
1 medium onion, very finely
    chopped
a pinch of powdered cinnamon
¼ cup rice or vermicelli
3 cups rich beef broth
juice of 1 lemon
1 tablespoon butter
chopped parsley, to garnish

Season the meat and knead it well. Add the onion and cinnamon and mix thoroughly. With moistened hands, roll the meat into marble-sized balls.

Boil the rice in some water until semi-cooked, then add the broth, meat balls, and lemon juice. Simmer together until the rice is tender, about 15 minutes. Cool.

Reheat just prior to serving, dot with the butter and sprinkle with the parsley. You could add a tablespoon or so of tomato purée or concentrate to vary this traditional soup from Jordan.

Lentil Soup

Serves 6:
1 large onion, finely chopped
½ stick butter
1¼ cup lentils, soaked
    overnight (canned will do)
5 cups beef broth, strained
1 teaspoon ground cumin
salt and freshly ground black
    pepper
2 tablespoons olive oil
¼ cup lemon juice
3 slices white bread, crusts
    removed, diced
1 clove garlic, crushed
finely chopped parsley, to
    garnish

Sauté the onion gently in half the butter until soft, then add the drained lentils and stir until glazed with the butter. Add the stock, cumin, salt and pepper and simmer until the lentils have almost disintegrated. Raw lentils will take 1½–2 hours; canned, about 50 minutes. Test the lentils to see whether they are tender, then cool and put the mixture briefly through a blender.

Fry the diced bread (or croûtons) in the remaining butter with the crushed garlic.

Return the soup to the pan, reheat, and simmer to boiling point. Stand on one side just before serving, and add the oil and lemon juice. Garnish with the croûtons and a little parsley.

*From Jordan, Feast-day soup
(left) is eaten on auspicious
occasions. Lentil soup (right)
enjoys wide popularity,
especially in Egypt and the
Levant – Lebanon, Syria and
Jordan.*

Vegetable Soup

Serves 6:

1 large onion, finely sliced
¼ cup olive oil
1 lb stewing beef, cubed
1 large potato, peeled and
  sliced
1 sweet red pepper, seeded and
  sliced
2 carrots, peeled and thinly
  sliced
½ cup plus 2 tablespoons
  shredded white cabbage
6 cups beef broth
tablespoon tomato concentrate
1 teaspoon dill
salt and pepper
2 tablespoons tarragon
  vinegar
finely chopped parsley, to
  garnish

Using a deep skillet, sauté the onion gently in the olive oil until it is soft. Add the meat, shaking the pan frequently to prevent the meat from sticking, and cook for 5 minutes. Add the vegetables and cook a further 10 minutes, turning frequently.

Transfer everything to a large, heavy based saucepan and add the broth, concentrate, dill and seasoning. Simmer gently on a low heat for 1-1½ hours.

Allow to cool, then remove the fat layer from the top. Reheat just before serving, adding the vinegar as a final touch. Garnish with the chopped parsley.

Eaten with chunks of bread, vegetable soup sustains many rural people for an entire day.

Zucchini Soup

Serves 4:
4 tablespoons olive oil
1 lb zucchini, washed, dried
   and thinly sliced
2 cloves garlic, crushed
1 large onion, thinly sliced
2½ cups fresh chicken broth
¼ cup finely chopped parsley
salt and freshly ground white
   pepper
2 teaspoons lemon juice

Heat the oil, add the zucchini, garlic and onion, and simmer for 10–15 minutes on a low heat. Add the broth, parsley and seasoning and simmer for 15 minutes.

Allow the soup to cool. Stir in the lemon juice and then purée the soup in a blender until almost smooth. Reheat without boiling and serve immediately.

Zucchini soup is very nourishing and simple to make.

Tomato Soup

Serves 6:

2 lbs medium tomatoes
1 clove garlic, finely chopped
1 medium onion, finely
  chopped
4 tablespoons olive oil
2½ cups chicken broth
a pinch of ground coriander
a pinch of paprika
salt and pepper to taste
juice of 1 lemon
finely chopped parsley, to
  garnish

Middle Eastern cooking uses only fresh ingredients: tomato soup.

Scald, peel and seed the tomatoes, then chop finely. Sauté the garlic, onions, coriander, paprika and seasonings in the olive oil until soft, then add the tomato pulp and cook 5 minutes.

Add the broth (use half this quantity of broth made up to 2½ cups with canned tomato juice, if desired). Cover and simmer 15–20 minutes. Cool the soup, then purée in a blender. Finally stir in the lemon juice, reheat and serve garnished with parsley.

Salads

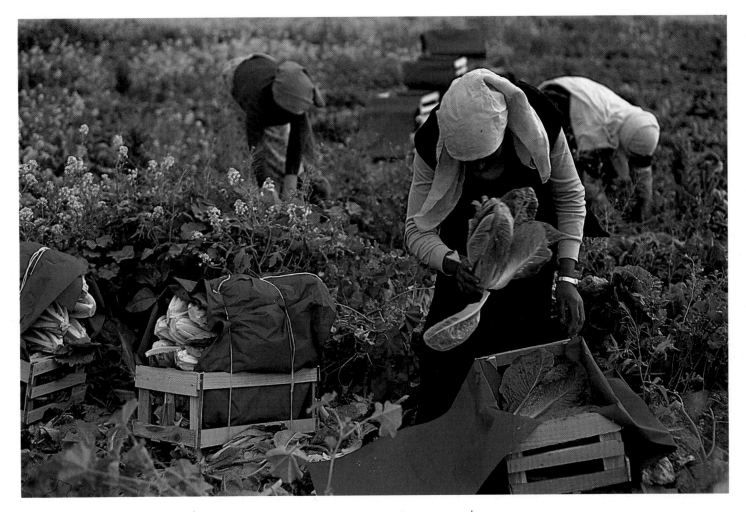

Harvesting lettuce in the Jordan Valley. Jordan grows most of its food requirements.

Some Middle Eastern countries are as much as two-thirds desert – where it may not rain for years – but revenues from oil and gas deposits, and ingenious irrigation techniques, enable even these places to cultivate vegetables.

Drip irrigation, where each plant has its own "dribble tap", means many of the arid Arabian Gulf states can grow luscious fruits and vegetables. Barren for thousands of years, the desert responds almost magically to water and fertilizers. Sustained on de-salinated water, cucumbers and cabbages grow twice as big as European strains and the tomato yield is prodigious.

In the Fertile Crescent, huge dams irrigate thousands of acres of previously arid countryside. In Syria, the Euphrates Dam has opened the dry eastern province of Raqqa to farming. I met Bedouin who had forsaken their nomadic existence to cultivate lettuces and other seedlings outside their tents.

In Jordan, water from the River Yarmuk is diverted through the East Ghor Canal from which feeder canals irrigate farms along the eastern bank of the River Jordan. The area crops two harvests a year, the entire family, even young children, turning out to help.

Crude farm tools in the National Museum in Baghdad attest to the early skills of Mesopotamian farmers. Iraq's largest flood control and irrigation system now centers on the Tharthar Reservoir which irrigates the arid plains north west of Baghdad.

But the greatest dam in the Middle East is the 12,230-foot-long Aswan Dam, in Egypt. The dam has made possible perennial irrigation all along the Nile Valley.

The Arab's fascination with water and his ability to utilize even the smallest amounts dates back some 3,000 years to when the ancient Egyptians built a vast dam across Wadi Gerrawi. Then, using neither mortar nor mechanization, the Sabaean Tribe in Southern Arabia built the giant Marib Dam in what is now known as North Yemen. Ancient texts say that the creation of the dam turned the district into a paradise. Strabo writes of abundant fruits and of great flocks of sheep in the meadows. The collapse of the dam inundated hundreds of miles of farmland and today Marib has been overtaken by seas of drifting sand, a wall and sluice gate being the only evidence of the dam's existence.

On the barren central plateau of Iran, farmers have for centuries cultivated by means of ingenious subterranean canals, or *kanats,* linking the strings of wells. Similar *falaj* or underground irrigation channels are found in al-Buraimi Oasis on the border of Abu Dhabi and the Sultanate of Oman.

So while some countries are still far from being self-sufficient, it is incorrect to only associate dates with the Arab World. Some of the sweetest, crispest salads I have ever eaten have been in the Middle East.

Salads like *tabbouleh* often come as appetizers. Otherwise, a fresh salad is invariably served with the main course.

As its name implies, *salata Arabieh* belongs to no particular country, but I always associate it with Lebanon. The freshly grilled fish, or charcoal broiled kebabs always arrived with a bowl of blood red tomatoes, peppermint green cucumbers and tangy onions from the Bekaa Valley, all shiny and inviting under a dressing of garlic, lemon juice and olive oil.

Fattouche, a popular Syrian peasant salad, uses crumbled bread as a variation on the theme. Additional flavors may include chopped fresh mint, parsley and coriander.

The recipe for tomato and coriander salad comes from Yemen, where local cooks have devised all kinds of highly original cold sauces and dips. I am partial to just a plain tomato and onion salad drenched in equal quantities of oil and lemon juice. White cheese, local bread and a tomato and onion salad became a favorite lunch when I stayed at the Winter Palace Hotel overlooking the Nile at Luxor in Egypt.

The use of yoghurt in salads is common in Middle Eastern cuisines, especially in Turkey and Jordan. Cucumber, nut and yoghurt salad is a wonderful summer appetizer. Another Turkish dish, eggplant salad, is one of my favorites. Cooked spinach also enjoys a close affinity with yoghurt, either plain or with garlic. Garlic, of course, is very much prized in the Middle East.

Kidney Bean Salad

Serves 4-6:
*1 can kidney beans, (or 1¼
    cup dried beans)*
juice of 1½-2 lemons
*¼ cup, plus 2 tablespoons
    olive oil*
salt and black pepper
1 sweet green pepper, chopped
6 scallions, finely chopped
1 tablespoon chopped parsley

If using dried kidney beans, allow to soak overnight in plenty of cold water, then wash and drain. Boil for 10 minutes, then simmer for 1½-2 hours until tender.

Drain the can of beans and prepare the dressing by mixing together the lemon juice, olive oil, salt and pepper. Pour over the beans, then mix in the green pepper, onions and parsley.

Line a bowl with lettuce leaves and tip in the bean salad. Garnish with a little more parsley.

Fattouche

Serves 4-6:

1 round stale Arab bread
1 cup coarsely chopped onion
4 scallions, coarsely chopped
    (optional)
1 cup chopped lettuce
½ cup finely chopped parsley
1 medium coarsely chopped
    cucumber
3 cups coarsely chopped
    tomatoes
1 tablespoon dried mint
juice of 2 large lemons
½ cup olive oil
salt and pepper to taste
2 cloves garlic, crushed

Break the
bread into small
pieces and put in
a large mixing bowl.
Add the chopped
onions, scallions, lettuce,
parsley, cucumber, tomatoes
and mint. Mix well, then leave the
bread to absorb the juices, about 10 minutes.
    Now make a dressing with the lemon
juice, olive oil and garlic. Season with salt
and black pepper and pour over the salad
mixture. Toss well and chill before serving.

Salata Arabieh

Serves 8:

6 medium tomatoes, diced
1 large cucumber, peeled and
   diced
2 medium onions, finely
   chopped
2 cloves garlic, finely chopped
1 medium sweet pepper,
   seeded and diced (optional)
1/4 cup chopped fresh mint
1/4 cup parsley, finely chopped
juice of 1 1/2-2 lemons
1/4 cup plus 2 tablespooons
   olive oil
salt and freshly ground black
   pepper

Combine all the vegetables
in a bowl. Mix the remaining
ingredients together and pour
over the vegetables. Toss very well
and chill before serving with Arab bread.

Cucumber and Raisin Salad with Yoghurt

Serves about 4:
3/4 cup plain yoghurt
1/4 cup raisins
1/4 cup chopped walnuts
2 scallions, finely chopped
a pinch of ground cumin
salt and freshly ground white
    pepper
2 medium cucumbers
2 tablespoons chopped fresh
    mint

Slice cucumber, sprinkle with salt and leave to drain in a colander for 30 minutes. Tip excess whey out of the yoghurt.

Combine the yoghurt, raisins, walnuts, scallions, cumin, salt and pepper in a bowl. Add the cucumber and mix well. Finally add the mint and chill prior to serving.

Eggplant Salad

Serves 6:
3 medium eggplants
salt
1/2 cup oil
3 cloves garlic, crushed
freshly ground black pepper
1/2 cup plain yoghurt
a pinch each of paprika and
    cumin

Cut the eggplants into 1/4 inch thick slices. Sprinkle with salt and leave for 30 minutes, weighted down with a flat dish to help remove the bitter juices. Rinse the eggplant slices and pat dry on paper towels.

Sauté the slices in hot oil until they are brown on both sides. Drain on kitchen paper.

Mix the garlic, salt and pepper into the yoghurt. Arrange layers of the eggplants in a flat serving dish and coat well with the yoghurt. Sprinkle with the paprika, chill and serve.

Spinach Salad

Serves 4:
1 lb fresh spinach
3/4 cup plain yoghurt
1 clove garlic, crushed
a pinch of cumin
salt and pepper

Clean the fresh spinach under running water and remove the stems and any large veins. Chop the leaves and simmer in their own juices until tender, about 20 minutes. Cool.

Drain excess whey off the yoghurt, then blend with the garlic, cumin and seasonings, add to the spinach and mix well. Chill until ready to serve.

Laced with yoghurt, cucumber (above left), eggplant (above right) and spinach (below) salads are especially popular in Turkey and Iran.

Tomato and Coriander Salad

Serves 4:
6 firm, ripe, medium tomatoes
½ bunch fresh coriander
leaves, chopped
a pinch of paprika
salt and freshly ground black
pepper
3 tablespoons olive oil
juice of 1 lemon

Scald, peel and slice the tomatoes into a bowl. Sprinkle with the chopped coriander leaves.

Combine the paprika, salt, pepper, oil and lemon juice, and beat vigorously. Pour over the tomatoes, then chill. Remove from the refrigerator 10 minutes before serving.

Green Pepper Salad

Serves 4:
4 medium green peppers
juice of 1½-2 lemons
¼ cup plus 2 tablespoons
olive oil
a dash of vinegar
1 clove garlic, crushed
salt to taste
black olives, to garnish

Quarter the sweet peppers lengthwise, and remove the seeds. Broil until the edges are brown and crisp. Allow to cool.

Make the dressing by mixing together the remaining ingredients, then pour over the peppers. Mix well, and garnish with one or two black olives.

Potato Salad

Serves 4-6:
2 lbs new potatoes, scrubbed
a good pinch of cumin
¼ cup, plus 2 tablespoons
olive oil
juice of 1½-2 lemons
3 cloves garlic, crushed
salt and pepper
4 tablespoons finely chopped
scallions
¼ cup finely chopped parsley

Boil the potatoes until they are just tender. Allow to cool a little, then peel and cut into uniform chunks. Sprinkle with cumin.

Prepare the dressing by mixing together the oil, lemon juice, garlic, salt and pepper. Pour over the potatoes. Toss well, chill until required, and serve garnished with the scallions and parsley.

Above right   *Green pepper or fil-fil salad*. Below left *Tomato and coriander salad from North Yemen*. Below right   *Potato salad*.

String Bean, Leek and Asparagus Salad

Serves 4:
1 lb chosen vegetable,
  prepared (see right)
1 clove garlic, crushed
¼ cup, plus 2 tablespoons
  olive oil
juice of 1½-2 lemons
salt and freshly ground black
  pepper

This salad can be made with any variety of green beans, leeks or asparagus. Top, tail and slice the beans; wash and slice the leeks; scrape the asparagus.

Cook each vegetable in a little salted water until barely tender, then drain and mix the remaining ingredients together and pour over the vegetables.

A Western touch is to garnish the leeks and the asparagus with chopped parsley and diced hard-boiled egg.

Vegetables and Rice

While the Western vogue for vegetarian cooking has only recently elevated vegetables to "main course" status, vegetables have a historically important position on a Middle Eastern menu. A frequently quoted saying during Abbasid times was: "A table without vegetables is like an old man devoid of wisdom."

Many dishes such as vegetable casserole are meals in themselves. So is stuffed eggplant, a great favorite of Abbasid society, the Caliph Wathiq being reportedly so fond of eggplant that he ate forty at a time. Iraqis transform the humble potato with a ground meat and pine nut filling, while the stuffed tomatoes of Egypt and the Levant have no equal.

While many Middle Eastern cities today have large, Western-style supermarkets, people still turn to the traditional *souqs* for buying fresh vegetables. Store owners display an artistic bent with colorful arrangements of polished tomatoes, shiny zucchinis, red and green peppers and purple eggplants. It is unthinkable not to be able to select your own vegetables, which are hunted down as soon as the *souq* opens. Usually the cook or a servant does the shopping, but in some countries it might be the grandmother with one of the servant's sons to carry her basket.

I especially remember an old Palestinian lady, possibly blind, groping slowly through the vegetable market in East Jerusalem. No doubt she knew her way and was probably a familiar figure, small, wrinkled and wearing a long, black robe. Stopping outside one shop, she felt around the display, then held up a smooth skinned eggplant, handing her purse trustingly to the owner for him to extract payment. While waiting, she popped a grape into her mouth; then smiling like a guilty child, she continued her shopping. I watched her buying a lettuce, lemons and bundles of coriander before losing sight of her in the crowds.

In conservative Arab states such as Qatar and Kuwait, it is common for men to do the shopping. By contrast, in Sana'a, well veiled women sell onions, carrots, tomatoes and other vegetables coaxed from the rocky soil.

The most commonly used Middle Eastern vegetables – zucchini, peppers, spinach and so on – are available in America. If you have trouble finding others such as okra, try a Greek store. Always bring home parsley to garnish dishes, and when cooking the Middle Eastern way, never be without a lemon.

Several recipes in this chapter are ideal for vegetarians: the popular *Imam bayıldı* (or swooning Imam), cabbage rolls, okra in oil and bean stew could make an entire buffet. Iran's contribution is an unusual combination of herbs and nuts in an omelet. Spinach is supposed to be native to Persia, but the recipe for spinach pie comes from Turkey, a delicious party dish which can be eaten hot or cold.

Wheat and rice are the main grains used in Middle Eastern cooking. Cracked wheat, or bulghur, is more usually

Right *A vegetable market in Dubai. Desert irrigation schemes enable many of the Gulf States to grow excellent vegetables.*

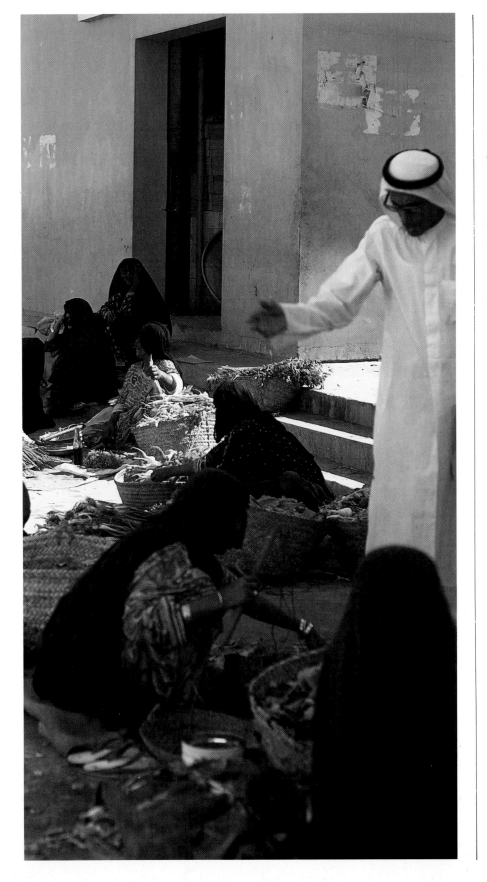

encountered in ground meat dishes, but it can be eaten plain with butter, topped with a fresh tomato purée or garlic flavored yoghurt with black pepper.

Rice is the basic dish throughout the Middle East: *roz* to the Arabs, *pilav* (cooked with other ingredients) in Turkey and *chelo* (steamed) or *polo* (cooked with other ingredients) in Iran. Basmati rice, which resembles the high grade Southern rice, is preferred, often colored by saffron or turmeric. Common ways of serving it are in a ring garnished with sauces and nuts. Meats and fish are frequently served on a bed of rice, a good example being the Bedouin whole roast lamb. Following a visit to Iran in 1971, I encountered *chelo*, a rice so subtle that I tend to make it to this day, the exception being saffron rice to serve with fish.

Last, but vital to millions of poorer people in the Middle East, are the dishes based on dried beans and peas: The bean dish, *foul medames*, is almost the national dish of Egypt. Most bean and pea recipes are geared to peasant taste – chick peas have already appeared in the guise of *hummus,* and there are recipes for lentil soup and lamb and chick pea casserole in the meat section.

We know that Middle Eastern cooks use a great deal of yoghurt. Plain, or spiked with garlic, it can be served with fried, sautéed or baked vegetables. Lemon juice is routinely used to heighten the flavor of many vegetable dishes such as cabbage rolls or baked eggplant with cumin.

Batata Charp *Stuffed Potatoes*

Serves 6:
8 medium potatoes
1 egg
2 tablespoons cornstarch
salt and pepper

Filling
4 tablespoons butter
1 medium onion, finely
 chopped
2 tablespoons cooking oil
a pinch each of paprika,
 ground cumin and allspice
½ lb lean beef, ground
1 cup cooking oil

First make the filling. Sauté the onion in the butter until golden and soft. Add the seasonings, then the meat. Cook for about 5 minutes until it changes color. Remove and set aside.

Peel and boil the potatoes. Mash well in a large bowl then add the egg, cornstarch, salt and pepper. Mix in very thoroughly. With moist hands break off a lump the size of a golf ball. Roll it in your hands, then flatten on your work surface and make a small hollow in the top. Fill this with a teaspoonful of the meat mixture and close the edges. Roll the potato ball around in your hand to ensure the meat is well sealed inside. Repeat this procedure until all the meat and potato is used up. Refrigerate the potato balls for at least 1 hour.

Heat the cup of cooking oil in a deep saucepan. When the oil is sizzling, gently lower a potato ball into the saucepan and cook quickly, turning on all sides until it is a golden brown. Cook each ball separately and be careful it does not break.

This amount makes about 15 potato balls. Serve with a chopped Arab salad, bread and a *labneh* dip.

Stuffed Tomatoes

Serves 2-4:
4 large firm tomatoes
salt and pepper
1 onion, finely chopped
¼ cup plus 2 tablespoons
 olive oil
¼ cup plus 2 tablespoons rice
pinch sugar
1 tablespoon currants
1 tablespoon pine nuts,
 chopped
1 tablespoon finely chopped
 mint
1 tablespoon finely chopped
 parsley

Select tomatoes of a uniform size. Carefully slice off the tops and set aside. Scoop out the pulp with a small spoon, removing any hard core, then chop the pulp. Sprinkle the inside of each tomato case with salt and pepper, and leave upside down to drain.

Sauté the onion gently in the olive oil until soft and golden. Add the tomato pulp, and the remaining ingredients, and simmer on a low heat for 3 minutes. Add a cup of water and cook gently until the rice softens, about 10 minutes.

Allow the mixture to cool, then spoon it into each tomato case, leaving enough room for the rice to swell. Top each tomato with its own "lid", and arrange side by side in an oiled baking dish. Brush each with a little extra oil and bake for 30 minutes in a moderate oven 325-350°F.

Imam Bayıldı *Baked Eggplant*

Serves 6:
3 medium eggplants
salt
¾ cup onion, finely chopped
½ cup olive oil
3 cloves garlic, crushed
1 small sweet red pepper,
  seeded and diced
5-6 medium tomatoes,
  skinned and finely chopped
2 tablespoons pine nuts,
  chopped
2 tablespoons raisins, chopped
½ teaspoon cayenne pepper
juice of 1 large lemon

Cut the eggplants in half lengthways. Using a serrated spoon, or similar, scoop out the flesh, being careful not to puncture the skin. Leave a case about ¼ inch thick. Chop and salt the pulp, place in a colander, and leave to drain for 1 hour. Rinse under cold running water then pat dry with paper towels. Rinse and dry the cases as well.

Fry the onion in some of the oil until it softens. Mix in the garlic and cook a further 3 minutes. Stir in the eggplant pulp, the sweet pepper and tomatoes, and cook on a medium heat until the pepper softens and most of the liquid has evaporated. Remove the pan from the heat and mix in the nuts, raisins, salt and cayenne pepper.

Preheat the oven to 350°F, and put the remaining oil in an ovenproof baking dish. Arrange the eggplant cases in it, in a close fitting layer. Fill each case with the stuffing and sprinkle with lemon juice. Gently add boiling water down one side of the baking dish to come about half-way up the eggplants. Cover with foil and bake in the oven for about 1 hour. Remove the dish when the cases are tender, and allow the eggplants to cool in the sauce.

When the eggplants are cold, drain off excess liquid and trickle a little extra olive oil over the cases. Chill until about 10 minutes before serving.

Stuffed vegetables are a feature of Middle Eastern cooking. Stuffed potatoes (above left) are a favorite in Iraq. Stuffed tomatoes (above right) may be eaten either hot or cold. Stuffed eggplant (below), here ready for the oven, is a medieval Turkish dish.

Baked Eggplant with Cumin

Serves 4:
2 lbs medium eggplants
6 cloves garlic, crushed
¼ cup plus 2 tablespoons
*   olive oil*
1 teaspoon paprika
1 heaped teaspoon ground
*   cumin*
2 pinches cayenne pepper
salt
lemon juice

Preheat the oven to 425–450°F.

Wash and dry the eggplants. Slit the skin in several places to prevent them bursting, then steam in a steamer until tender, about 30–40 minutes (in a pressure cooker, about 12–15 minutes). Allow to cool, then cut each eggplant into three pieces lengthways. Sprinkle with the garlic.

Heat the oil in an ovenproof dish in the oven. Put the eggplants in and sprinkle with the paprika, cumin, cayenne pepper

and a little salt. Bake 5 minutes in the hot oven.

Just before serving, sprinkle with a few drops of fresh lemon juice.

Baked eggplant sprinkled
with cumin is a common
Middle Eastern recipe. Dip
Arab bread into the sauce.

Cabbage Rolls

Serves 8-10:
20 cabbage leaves

Stuffing
½ cup rice
4 tablespoons olive oil
*2 medium onions, finely
    chopped*
2 cloves garlic, crushed
2 tablespoons pine nuts
*½ lb lean ground beef, or
    lamb*
*3 medium tomatoes, finely
    chopped*
½ teaspoon cumin
½ teaspoon allspice
1 tablespoon dried mint
lemon juice

First make the stuffing. Cook the rice in boiling water for about 8 minutes. Drain. Sauté the onions, garlic and pine nuts until golden, then add the ground meat, stir well and cook until it changes colour. Add tomatoes, mint, cumin and allspice and simmer the mixture for a further 5 minutes. Keep warm.

Choose large, whole fresh cabbage leaves. Plunge into boiling salted water to make them pliable, then spread on a wooden board and cut out the core, and hard veins. Place a portion of stuffing on each leaf and roll into a neat packet.

Place the rolls close together in a shallow casserole dish and add enough salted water, or broth to almost cover. Make sure they are tightly packed or they might unwrap. Cover and cook in a moderate oven (350–375°F) for about 40 minutes, or until tender.

Serve hot sprinkled with fresh lemon juice, or a sauce made from fresh tomatoes and cream – as preferred.

Stuffed and spiced, the humble cabbage is elevated to almost regal status.

String Bean Stew

Serves 6:
2 lbs string beans
Tomato Sauce
3 cloves garlic, crushed
½ teaspoon ground coriander
3 tablespoons olive oil
2 tablespoons tomato
　concentrate
2 medium onions, chopped
6 medium tomatoes, skinned
1 tablespoon chopped parsley
salt and white pepper
½ teaspoon paprika
juice of 1 lemon

First, prepare the tomato sauce. Sauté the garlic and coriander in the oil, then add the onions and cook the mixture for 10 minutes. Add the tomato concentrate, tomatoes and parsley and crush and blend into a purée. Mix in the salt, pepper, paprika and lemon juice and simmer uncovered for 15 minutes. Stir frequently to make a rich, aromatic sauce.

Trim the beans as necessary and place in a large saucepan or casserole dish with the sauce and enough water to barely cover. Simmer until tender (about 15 minutes).

If you prefer your beans *al dente*, remove after 10 minutes and set aside while you reduce the sauce to a thicker consistency. Return the beans and reheat to serve.

Zucchini with Tomatoes

Serves 4:
2 lbs zucchini
2 cloves garlic, crushed
a pinch of ground coriander
4 tablespoons olive oil
6 medium tomatoes
salt and black pepper
2 tablespoons chopped parsley

Wash and dry the zucchini, and slice into moderately thick rounds.

Sauté the garlic and coriander in the oil, then add the zucchini slices. Cook gently for about 10 minutes, turning frequently.

Add the tomatoes, peeled and chopped, salt, pepper and parsley, and simmer until cooked, about 20 minutes. Serve hot.

Okra Stew

Serves 4:

6 medium tomatoes, sliced
1 lb fresh okra
cider vinegar
3 cloves garlic, crushed
2 medium onions, finely
    chopped
1 teaspoon coriander
2 tablespoons olive oil
salt and pepper
1 tablespoon tomato
    concentrate
ground cumin
juice of 1 lemon

String bean stew (below left), zucchini with tomatoes (below right) and okra or bamieh (right) are favorite vegetable dishes in the Middle East.

Scald, skin and slice the tomatoes. Wash and cut off the okra stems, taking care not to puncture the pods. Soak okra for 30 minutes in vinegar to prevent them becoming sticky during cooking. Drain and rinse under running water.

Sauté the garlic, coriander and onions in the olive oil until soft. Place half in a greased ovenproof dish, and top with a layer of sliced tomato. Make second layers of onion and tomato, then arrange the okra on top. Season and top with the remaining tomatoes.

Mix tomato concentrate with a little water, pour over the vegetables, then add enough water to almost cover them. Add a good pinch of cumin and cook for 10 minutes over a high heat.

Remove from the heat, add lemon juice and bake in a moderate oven 350–375°F until the okra are tender (about 1 hour). By now the liquid will have reduced by a third. Serve hot in the casserole dish.

Herb and Nut Omelet

Serves 4:
4 tablespoons butter
6 scallions, finely chopped
2 lettuce leaves, finely
  chopped
1 teaspoon dried dill (or 3
  tablespoons fresh dill weed)
¼ cup plus 2 tablespoons
  chopped parsley
8 eggs
saffron to color, or ¼ teaspoon
  turmeric
a pinch of cinnamon
salt and pepper
a pinch of baking soda
¼ cup raisins, roughly chopped
¼ cup walnuts, chopped

Melt half the butter in a deep ovenproof skillet. Add the scallions, lettuce, dill and parsley and sauté until the scallions are transparent. Add the remaining butter and allow to melt.

Preheat the oven to 350°F.

Beat the eggs well, then add saffron (or turmeric), cinnamon, salt and pepper and baking soda. Stir in the raisins and nuts. Now add this to the mixture in the skillet but do not stir. Transfer skillet to the preheated oven and bake until golden and set.

Serve immediately, either alone or with a tomato salad.

Ideal for vegetarians, a magically flavored herb and nut omelet from Persia.

Baked Squash in Tahini Sauce

Serves 4-6:
4 medium yellow squash
½ stick butter
*3 medium onions, finely
  chopped*
4 cloves garlic, crushed
pepper
½ teaspoon ground coriander
½ teaspoon paprika
¼ teaspoon ground cinnamon
*1 lb lean lamb or beef, finely
  ground*
salt
½ cup tahini (sesame seed paste)
*¼ cup plus 2 tablespoons
  lemon juice, or more*
½ cup pine nuts (or walnuts)

Peel the squash and slice into rounds about ½ inch thick. Sauté in the butter until almost cooked and golden brown. Set aside.

In the same pan, sauté the onions and half of the crushed garlic. Season with pepper, coriander, paprika and cinnamon, then add the meat and cook until lightly brown. Add salt.

Line a greased casserole dish with a layer of closely packed squash, spread the meat mixture over it, then layer with remaining squash.

Blend the *tahini*, lemon juice, remaining garlic and salt to taste in a bowl. Blend to the consistency of half and half, adding more lemon juice if necessary. Pour this into the casserole and bake in a moderate oven (375°F) until the top turns a golden brown (about 40 minutes).

*Baked squash with tahini is a
tasty recipe from Lebanon.*

Turkish Vegetable Casserole

Serves about 6-8:

1 medium eggplant, sliced
salt
4 medium okra, about 3
*   inches long*
2 medium onions, chopped
1 sweet green pepper, seeded
*   and chopped*
4 medium zucchini, unpeeled
*   and coarsely chopped*
1 cup dwarf string beans
1 cup green peas
1 lb potatoes, peeled and cubed
4 cloves garlic, crushed
1 bunch of parsley, finely
*   chopped*
2 teaspoons paprika
1 heaped teaspoon ground
*   cumin*
5-6 medium tomatoes, peeled
*   and sliced*
6-8 tablespoons olive oil
1 teaspoon sugar

Soak the eggplant slices in salted water for 30 minutes; remove and drain well. Prepare okra as for Okra Stew (page 71).

Sauté the onion in a little of the oil until soft and golden. Transfer to a casserole dish and add the remaining vegetables, except the tomatoes. Add the garlic, parsley and all the seasonings, 2 cups of water (or broth), and most of the olive oil. Mix together, then add the tomatoes and dribble in the remaining olive oil. Finally flatten the vegetables down with a wooden spoon.

Simmer for about 1 hour, covered, in a moderate oven (375°F), or until the

vegetables are tender. Remove the casserole, add salt to taste and the sugar, stir well and cook a further 15-20 minutes.

Serve the vegetable casserole with bread as a hot dip. The Turks also like *turlu guvec* cold.

Rich Turkish vegetable casserole or turlu guvec.

Far right   *Spinach pie is a Turkish favorite. It makes an excellent party dish eaten hot, or cold.*

Spinach Pie

Serves 6–8:
12 sheets filo pastry
1 cup olive oil

Filling
2½ lbs fresh spinach (or
frozen spinach, thawed)
salt and pepper
¾ cup onions, chopped
2 tablespoons butter
4 large eggs, beaten
½ lb Feta cheese (or Cheddar
and Parmesan)
2 teaspoons dried dill weed
1 heaped teaspoon paprika

First prepare the filling. If using fresh spinach, wash it, remove the stalks and any large veins, and cut the leaves into thin strips. Sprinkle with salt and leave for 1 hour. Then rub the leaves and squeeze out all the liquid. Follow package instructions for frozen spinach.

Sauté the onions in the butter until transparent. Add onions, beaten eggs, cheese, dill and paprika to the spinach and mix well. Add salt and pepper to taste.

Heat the oven to moderate, 350°F. Grease a 10 × 12 inch baking pan.

Brush one side of one sheet of the pastry with oil and lay it in the tin – which it will overlap. Brush five more sheets individually with oil and place on top. Now place the spinach filling on this and trickle 2 tablespoons olive oil over it.

Bring the overlapping pastry up over the filling. Cut the last six sheets to the size of the tin, brush them individually with oil and lay them on top.

Score the top with squares and sprinkle with water to prevent the edges curling. Bake in the oven until the top is a golden brown, about 30–45 minutes.

Saffron Rice

Serves 4:
1½ cup rice
4 tablespoons pine nuts
3 tablespoons olive oil
3 medium onions, finely
*   chopped*
3 tablespoons raisins
1 teaspoon salt
enough saffron to color, or ½
*   teaspoon turmeric*

Wash and soak the rice for 2 hours. Rinse in a sieve under running water until clear, then drain. Brown the pine nuts in the oil, then add the onions and sauté them until soft and golden. Divide this mixture in half.

Add the raisins and one half of the mixture to the rice together with the salt and saffron or turmeric. Bring 3 cups of water to the boil, add the rice etc., and stir for 1 minute on a medium heat. Reduce the heat, and simmer until the water is absorbed, about 15-20 minutes. Stir in the rest of the onions and pine nuts, mix well, and serve immediately.

Plain Pilaf Rice

Serves 2-3:
1 cup long-grain rice
2 tablespoons butter,
*   or 2 tablespoons oil*
salt

Wash the rice in a sieve under running water until it is clear. Soak for 2 hours in cold water, then drain.

Boil 1 cup water, and add the butter (or oil), salt and rice. Bring back to the boil, stir well, cover and cook for 15-20 minutes. To color, add several strands of saffron, or ½ teaspoon of turmeric, to the water.

Chelo *Persian Steamed Rice*

Serves 4:
1½ cups Basmati rice
3 tablespoons melted butter
1 tablespoon salt

Wash rice in boiling water then soak in salted water for 6 hours. Rinse the rice in a sieve under running water until it is clear. Place in a pan, add a pinch of salt, cover with boiling water and cook vigorously for 10 minutes. Wash and drain again.

To steam the rice, heat ½ cup of cold water and 2 tablespoons butter in a saucepan. Add the rice, smoothing it flat. Fold a clean dish towel in half and place it over the top of the saucepan then cover with the lid. The dish towel will trap and absorb the steam, helping the rice to remain fluffy.

After 15 minutes, the rice should be ready. Trickle the remaining butter over it and serve. Persians serve an egg yolk in a hollow made in each portion of *chelo*.

Three different rices – chelo or Persian steamed rice (center), plain boiled rice pilaf (top) and saffron rice (right) for serving with fish. A raw egg yolk, butter and spices are mixed into the chelo for eating with kebabs in Iran.

Meat

My first taste of Middle Eastern cookery came in Aden, now capital of the Democratic Republic of South Yemen. In 1963, a passenger liner bearing me and several hundred other young Australians called at Aden on her three and a half week voyage to Europe.

Tired of shipboard food, we had streamed ashore in search of something fresh when the odor of grilling meat drew me into a small restaurant. Surrounded by curious men, I had my first taste of *kebabs* and while I have subsequently eaten them from Casablanca to Peshawar, I still remember this simple dish, and the cook polishing my knife and fork on his apron.

Shish kebab, to use the full name, is credited with being a Turkish creation. The story goes that, obliged to camp out during the Ottoman conquests, Turkish soldiers adopted the habit of cooking skewered meat – goat, lamb, gazelle and so on – over an open fire outside their tents. In fact, it could just as easily have been devised by invading Persian or Mongol tribes.

On the subject of *kebabs*, the most important considerations are to purchase a good cut of meat and to marinate it for at least three to four hours. I usually mix a marinade made from the juice of two large onions, a half cup of olive oil, a heaped teaspoon of oregano, a pinch of cayenne pepper, plus salt and freshly ground black pepper, and refrigerate the meat in it overnight in a covered bowl. When grilling *kebabs*, or any other meat, fish or poultry, wait until the

charcoal has ceased smoking before you start cooking. Using a broiler, cook quickly under a high heat to seal the juices, then brown the outside. The cooking time will depend on how well you like your meat done.

The ways of cooking meat in the Middle East are basically the same as in the West: grilling (as in *kebabs*),

Sizzling kebabs cooked at a roadside stall by the Desert Highway in Jordan.

Döner kebap has travelled the world with Turkish migrants. The cooked lamb is carved into a pocket of bread with salad and spices.

stewing and roasting. Ground meat dishes are very popular in the Levant and Syria in particular, where women vie with each other to produce the finest *kibbeh*.

The Arabs tend to eat more grilled meats, such as *kebabs* and lamb roasted on a spit. *Yaknéh*, or meat and vegetable stews, are

common in the Levant. The Yemenis, too, are fond of stews, a popular ingredient being okra; okra (*bamieh*) is also a traditional dish in Egypt. Some Middle Eastern stews have an earthy, rather peasant-type texture – like the lamb and chick pea casserole. The more refined Persian taste, which permeates all types of local cooking, is found in the veal and prune casserole dish, a fascinating blend of "sweet and sour" ingredients.

Stews are normally simmered a long time on the stove. Alternatively, if the ingredients have been sealed by frying, or sautéeing, they are baked in the oven.

With people always running in and out of the kitchen, servants, grandmothers and friends to help, there is always someone to watch a meal cooking in a Middle Eastern household.

So often discarded in the West, bones are greatly prized for the marrow, a cracked bone added to a stew for extra richness. Unlike meat for grilling, you can buy cheaper cuts for a stew. Searing meats in oil, or butter, traps the juices and adds a richer color to the dish. Simmering the meat, as in many Persian recipes, makes for a light, almost insipid looking stew which is then enriched with spices, nuts and fruits. Most Middle Eastern cooks find it difficult to be precise about quantities; they tend to cook by heart with constant tastings and adjustings.

Organs are revered as we have seen with brains, liver and fries in the chapter on *mezze*. I have marvelous memories of brains served in the Oriental buffet at the Hilton Hotel in al-Ain, the large oasis town in inland Abu Dhabi. I have eaten kidneys just about everywhere. Up early to photograph Shibam, a mountain town outside Sana'a, my driver and I had liver for breakfast. Served with a bowl of *foul* and flat

wholewheat bread, it is a specialty of Yemeni mountain towns on market day. Fries, as lamb's testicles are called, are more rare. I have only ever eaten them in Lebanon and in Lebanese restaurants in London. They are of a taste and texture similar to sweetbreads and you should have your butcher prepare them as they are rather messy.

Lamb or mutton is the most commonly used meat throughout the Middle East. Goat is also eaten by the Bedouin, and I once came upon a wedding in Abu Dhabi when a young camel had been slain and was cooking in an enormous pot of stew.

The roast stuffed lamb makes a nice Sunday dinner. You can use either a leg or a shoulder for for the lamb, yoghurt and lemon recipe or *kharouf bi limoun* as it is known in Arabic. I have cooked this time and time again with unfailingly excellent results. Easily prepared, it is a good choice if expecting guests on a week night. I serve it with boiled new potatoes liberally sprinkled with cumin, and either cold bean salad or a green salad.

Of the other recipes, the okra stew recipe comes from Jordan; lamb and chick pea casserole is found throughout the Middle East (especially in Egypt when people can afford the meat); Syrian meatloaf is a useful dish – eat it hot first, then serve it cold with a salad; and I often cook *Lady's Thighs* to serve as appetizers at a cocktail party. They can be made before the guests arrive and kept warm in the oven.

Persian Casserole with Prunes

Serves about 6:
24 prunes
3 lbs veal, cut into cubes
salt and pepper to taste
1 teaspoon ground cumin
juice of 3 lemons
½ cup cooking oil
4 tablespoons flaked almonds
½ stick butter
2 medium onions, chopped
4½ cups stock
2 tablespoons powdered sugar

Soak the prunes overnight. Marinate the meat together with the seasonings in half the lemon juice and the oil. Leave for 2 hours. While the meat is marinating, brown the almonds on baking sheet and set aside.

Melt the butter in a deep skillet and sauté the onion until soft. Drain the meat, add it to the skillet and brown on all sides. Add the stock, cover the skillet and simmer on a low heat for about 1½ hours, or until tender. To reduce the amount of stock, cook uncovered for the final 30 minutes.

Drain the prunes, keeping 1 cup of juice. Mix the powdered sugar with juice and transfer to a large pan. Simmer gently for 15 minutes. Meanwhile remove the pits from the prunes.

When the meat is cooked, remove the skillet from the heat, add the prunes, the prune juice, half the almonds and the rest of the lemon juice. Stir this in, and cook rapidly for 5 minutes. Remove from the heat and sprinkle with the remaining almonds. Serve with *chelo* rice (see page 76) and a green salad.

Roast Stuffed Neck of Lamb

Serves 4-6:
*2-3 lbs boned neck of lamb
Juice of 2 medium onions
1 tablespoon ground coriander
1 teaspoon ground ginger
salt and freshly ground black
    pepper
2 tablespoons oil*

Stuffing
*1 cup rice
saffron to color, or ½ teaspoon
    turmeric
2 onions, chopped
¼ cup pine nuts (or blanched
    almonds)
½ teaspoon allspice
½ stick butter
½ cup golden raisins
salt and black pepper*

Wipe the inside and outside of the neck with a cloth, rub well with onion juice and seasonings and set aside.

To prepare the stuffing, cook the rice until it is light and fluffy. Sauté the onions, pine nuts and allspice in the butter, then mix with the rice. Add the golden raisins, mix well and season with salt and pepper. Leave to cool.

Pack the stuffing into the meat and secure with strong string. Rub with half the oil, then sear in the remaining oil in a hot oven 425-450°F.

Cook for 15 minutes, turning on all sides, then reduce the heat to moderate (375°F). Roast at this heat, turn once again, then allow to become crisp. As for other lamb dishes, cooking time will depend on how you like your meat – whether pink or well done. Allow about 30 minutes per ½ pound weight.

Shoulder of Lamb with Saffron

Serves 4:

3 whole cloves garlic, peeled
2½ lbs shoulder of lamb
1 teaspoon mixed herbs
salt and pepper
½ cup olive oil
2 onions, sliced
juice of 2 lemons
a pinch of cayenne pepper
saffron, to color

Chop the garlic into slivers and insert in small cuts all over the lamb. Mix the herbs, salt, pepper and half the oil and marinate the lamb for 2 hours.

In a deep skillet, sauté the onion in the remaining oil until golden brown, then add the juice of 1 lemon, season with cayenne pepper, and simmer for 5 minutes. Remove to a casserole dish.

Now heat the marinating oil in the skillet, add the shoulder and sear on all sides. Add the juice of the second lemon mixed with the saffron and transfer to the casserole dish. Cook in a moderate oven until tender, about 1½-2 hours.

Serve the lamb, carved into slices, garnished with sliced lemon and accompanied by rice.

Roast Leg of Lamb with Yoghurt and Lemon

Serves 6-8:
1 leg of lamb, about
    4lbs in weight
salt and freshly ground black
    pepper
4 cloves garlic
olive oil
½ cup lemon juice, plus a
    little grated lemon rind
1 cup plain yoghurt

Season the lamb well with salt and black pepper. Cut the garlic into small slivers and insert in cuts all over the leg. Set aside for 4 hours. Preheat the oven to 450°F.

Heat ½ cup of oil in a roasting dish in the oven until it sizzles, and sear the lamb on all sides, about 15 minutes. Remove from the oven and allow to cool slightly, then pour over half the lemon juice, the rind and half the yoghurt. Reduce the oven heat to about 375°F.

Replace the lamb in the oven and bake, turning once and adding more lemon juice and yoghurt. Add water if the lemon juice dries up. Do not turn after the final hour, to allow the yoghurt to form a golden brown crust.

Serve this crusty tender lamb in slices, with boiled new potatoes and cumin, and any of the green or tomato salads.

Okra and Lamb Stew

Serves 4-5:
1½ lbs young okra
vinegar
3 cloves garlic, crushed
1 teaspoon ground coriander
2 tablespoons butter
2 lbs lean lamb, cubed
6 medium ripe tomatoes (or
  10 oz can with juice),
  chopped
1½ cups rich broth
salt and freshly ground black
  pepper
2 tablespoons lemon juice

Wash the okra and cut off the stems, taking care not to puncture the pods. Soak pods in vinegar for 30 minutes, then drain and dry on a paper towel.

Sauté the garlic and coriander in the butter in a large saucepan or casserole dish, then add the lamb and seal over a high flame. Turn each piece until it changes color, then add the okra and tomatoes. Simmer for 5-10 minutes, then cover with the broth. Season with salt and pepper, stir well, and simmer on a low heat for 1½-2 hours, or until tender. By this time the sauce should be greatly reduced. Add the lemon juice just before serving.

Okra stew is a favorite in Jordan. Okra and lentils are two of the most common stew ingredients in the Middle East.

Lamb and Chick Pea Casserole

Serves 4-5:
1 lb dried chick peas
3 cups water
1 large onion, chopped
4 cloves garlic, finely chopped
1 teaspoon ground allspice
1 teaspoon paprika
a pinch of ground cumin
salt and freshly ground black
　pepper
1 lb small eggplants
3 lbs boned lamb cut into
　pieces
1 shin bone with marrow,
　chopped in 2-3 pieces
6 tablespoons olive oil
2 tablespoons lemon juice
¾ cup tahini (seasame seed
　paste)

Soak the chick peas overnight in cold water, then drain.

Put the 3 cups of water in a deep heavy casserole. Add the onion, garlic, chick peas and seasonings. Trim the lamb well, add to the casserole, cover and simmer for about 2 hours.

When the meat is tender, remove from the stove and allow to cool. Extract the marrow and discard the large bones. Chill the dish while preparing the eggplants.

Soak the eggplants for 30 minutes in cold, salted water, then drain well, pat dry and slice thinly. Heat the olive oil in a skillet and fry each piece a golden brown. Drain on paper towels and keep warm.

Remove the casserole from the refrigerator and skim the fat off the surface. Add more salt if necessary, plus a liberal amount of black pepper, and reheat in the oven. Now blend the lemon juice and *tahini* and add to the casserole. Stir in and simmer gently for 10 minutes. Invert the casserole into a serving dish, add the eggplants and keep in the oven until read to serve – about 10 minutes.

Serve with Arab bread to mop up the rich sauce, and a chopped salad.

Lamb and chick pea casserole topped with sliced eggplant. A substantial meal on a cold night.

Braised Chops with Vegetables

Serves 4:
yellow squash, zucchini, leek
    (or vegetable of choice),
    sliced
8-10 fleshy lamb chops
2 tablespoons butter
1 large onion, sliced
2-3 cloves garlic, chopped
a generous pinch each of
    coriander, paprika and
    allspice
6 medium ripe tomatoes,
    sliced
¼ cup finely chopped parsley
salt and freshly ground black
    pepper
¾ cup broth

*Braised chops with vegetables
is widely eaten, especially in
rural areas.*

Use 1–2 medium yellow squash, or 2 large
zucchini, or about 1 lb leeks.

Trim the chops of any excess fat and
brown in butter on both sides. Remove
from the skillet and place in a greased
ovenproof dish. Preheat the oven to 375°F.

Sauté the onion, garlic and spices in
butter remaining in skillet until soft. Add
the tomatoes, half the parsley and the salt
and pepper. Simmer for 10 minutes, then
add the broth, mixing thoroughly.

Place the sliced vegetables on top of the
chops, and pour the sauce mixture over
them. Add more seasoning, as desired.
Cook in the oven until the chops are tender
and the sauce is rich and aromatic. Garnish
with the remaining parsley. Serve with

potato purée, or with baked potatoes,
slashed open and garnished with butter and
cumin.

Meatballs in Yoghurt Sauce

Serves 4:
2 lbs lean beef, finely ground
*½ cup bulghur or cracked
    wheat, soaked and dried*
*a pinch each of paprika and
    allspice*
*3 medium onions, very finely
    ground*
½ cup pine nuts
salt and freshly ground pepper
2 tablespoons butter
cooking oil

Yoghurt sauce
1½ cups plain yoghurt
1 tablespoon cornstarch
salt and pepper to taste
2-3 cloves crushed garlic
½ cup dried mint, crushed

*Meatballs with yoghurt sauce
is served by most Syrian and
Lebanese restaurants. It is
eaten with rice and a salad.*

Mix together the meat, bulghur and spices as per the instructions for *kibbeh nayé* on page 35. Meanwhile sauté the onion and pine nuts lightly in the butter and allow to cool.

Break off lumps of meat the size of a golf ball and stuff with the pine nut and onion mixture. Heat the oil in a deep saucepan and fry the meatballs until crisp on the outside, but juicy within. Drain on a piece of kitchen paper and keep warm.

To stabilise the yoghurt, pour it into a large saucepan and beat until liquid. Mix the cornstarch with a little water to make a paste. Add this to the yoghurt together with a pinch of salt. Heat to just below boiling while stirring continuously in one direction. Continue to stir the mixture on a minimum heat, or until the sauce thickens. Do not cover, or overheat.

While making the yoghurt sauce, sauté the garlic in a little butter, add the mint and mix this into the yoghurt sauce. Season further according to your own taste.

Place the meatballs in a serving dish and cover with the sauce. Serve with plain rice and chopped Arab salad, with bread to mop up the sauce.

Syrian Stuffed Kibbeh

Serves 4:
kibbeh recipe (page 35),
    using ½ cup bulghur
oil

Filling
1 *medium onion, finely diced*
¼ *cup pine nuts*
½ *stick butter, or more*
½ *lb lamb, very finely ground*
½ *teaspoon allspice*
salt and freshly ground
    black pepper

Make the *kibbeh* mixture first.
    To make the filling, sauté the onion and pine nuts in the butter. When they turn golden brown, toss the meat and allspice in the pan, cooking lightly until the meat changes color. Add salt and pepper and mix well. While this cools, prepare the *kibbeh* shells.

The Syrians are masters at making kibbeh, the pounding of the mince and burghul being a familiar sound. Pictured on the right is stuffed kibbeh served with hummus and muhammara dips.

Break off a lump the size of a small egg and, cupping it in your palm, make a hole in the center with your finger. Mold the paste around your finger, working up and down and round and round (a practice likened by Middle Eastern cookery expert, Claudia Roden, to pottery making). It is a difficult art: if the paste breaks, use moistened hands to stick it together again.
    Now fill each egg shaped *kibbeh* with a

little stuffing. Seal the edges by wetting with iced water. As each *kibbeh* is made, set it aside on a tray (you can prepare them in advance and chill them).

Heat a deep skillet with enough oil to cover the *kibbeh*. When the oil is sizzling, drop them in and cook on a high heat, turning frequently until they turn rich brown but the filling remains juicy. Drain on kitchen paper and serve either hot or cold, with a selection of dips and salads.

Ground Meat Kebabs

Serves 6:
2 lbs lean lamb or beef, ground
3 medium onions, finely
chopped
¾ cup parsley, coarsely
chopped
salt and freshly ground black
pepper
½ teaspoon allspice
½ teaspoon cayenne pepper
oil
flour

Put the meat through a food processor. When well kneaded, add the finely chopped onion, parsley, salt and spices to the meat mixture.

With moistened hands, break off walnut-sized lumps of the mixture and mold around a skewer (you'll need six). Place two sausage-shaped amounts on each skewer. Dust with flour to hold firmly, then brush lightly with oil and broil over a charcoal fire. Use a high heat and turn frequently.

Place on a bed of lettuce garnished with lemon wedges and *hummus* or *muhammara*

(see pages 24 and 28) side dips and serve with rice and salad.

Serve ground meat kebabs with a dip like hummus or muhammara or babagannouj.

Turkish-style Kebabs

The sizzle of grilling kebabs is music to the ears. Turkish-style kebabs.

Allow ½ lb meat per person, to make two skewers each. Choose a good cut of meat – lamb or beef – and cut it into chunky cubes. Rub with salt and freshly ground black pepper and marinate in lemon juice, olive oil and marjoram for about 2 hours. (To make the *kebabs* more piquant, add a good pinch of paprika to the marinade.)

Cut up chunks of green or red pepper, onions and firm tomatoes to intersperse with the meat. Halved kidneys are even more delicious.

Impale the meat, onions, tomato and chunks of pepper alternately on the skewers and broil under a high heat, turning frequently until cooked on all sides.

Serve on the skewers with plain rice. Side dips are *hummus*, *muhammara* and *labneh*.

Syrian Meatloaf

Serves about 6-8:
¼ cup pine nuts
butter
2 eggs
2 medium onions, finely
   chopped
2 inch piece of fresh ginger,
   grated
3 tablespoons tomato purée
   (canned will do)
1 teaspoon ground allspice
salt and freshly ground black
   pepper
2 lbs good quality lamb,
   ground
¾ cup fresh breadcrumbs
lemon wedges, cress or
   parsley, to garnish

First sauté the pine nuts lightly in a little butter and set aside

In a mixing bowl beat the eggs, then add the onions, grated ginger and other seasonings. Mix well.

Knead the ground lamb thoroughly. Make a hole in the center of the mixture. Pour in the egg mixture, add the pine nuts and make sure everything is very well mixed. Finally add the fresh breadcrumbs to bind the mixture. Form into a loaf shape, and sprinkle with a little cold water and a dot of butter. Wrap in foil and bake about 1–1½ hours in a preheated oven 375°F. Unwrap the foil for the final 30

minutes to allow to brown.

Syrian meatloaf may be served either hot or cold. This recipe leaves enough over to use cold; it is a good picnic dish. Serve with side dishes of *labneh* and salad.

Syrian meatloaf can be eaten hot or cold. Serve with a labneh dip and a lettuce salad.

Kidneys in Tomato Sauce

Serves 4:
12 lamb's kidneys
lemon juice or vinegar
2 onions, finely chopped
2 cloves garlic, crushed
a pinch each of chili powder,
   ground coriander and
   cumin, and chopped
   parsley
2 tablespoons butter
4 medium tomatoes, skinned
   and pulped
1 tablespoon tomato paste
salt and freshly ground black
   pepper

Soak the kidneys in water with 2 teaspoons of lemon juice or vinegar, for about 2 hours. Drain, skin, slice in half and remove the cores. Cut into quarters.

Sauté the onion, garlic and seasonings in the butter. Add the kidneys and toss lightly until they change color in the skillet. Add the tomato pulp and paste, mixing well. Finally add the salt and pepper, and a little water rinsed in the dish which contained the concentrate.

Cook gently on a low heat, about 10–15 minutes, according to how you like kidneys done. Serve with plain rice and a green salad.

Kidneys in tomato sauce. Offal is widely enjoyed throughout the Middle East. Yemenis eat liver and kidneys for breakfast.

Poultry Dishes

One medieval Middle Eastern recipe book lists over 300 different ways of cooking poultry, especially chicken. Apparently Kaskari chickens (Kaskar is a village between the Tigris and the Euphrates) were considered to have the best taste and, according to one translator, they grew "as heavy as a goat, or a sheep". The breeding of chickens appears to have been common at this time, yet it was not so long ago, especially in the Arab countries, that chickens were so scarce they were considered a luxury.

I recall an incident during travels through North Yemen when, invited to eat at a rural dwelling, I was sitting talking to my host. A terrible squawking came from below and peering out a window, I saw a boy chasing a scraggy hen until, with a well aimed stick, he

Chickens are in for a rough ride in North Yemen. More than 300 different ways of cooking poultry exist in the Middle East.

killed it. The fact that it was his father's only chicken underlined the family's incredible hospitality. Now ironically, like most Middle Eastern towns, Sana'a has a "Kentucky Fried Chicken" restaurant (although it was closed for months as the owner was rumored to be a Jew)!

It is probably true that there are more ways of cooking poultry than any other ingredient in the Middle Eastern repertoire. Recipes in this chapter range from chicken *kebab* (cover) to the exotic duckling in walnut and pomegranate sauce. Finding we were only two one Christmas, I cooked Persian chicken (stuffed with apricots, prunes, raisins and pine nuts) which was as good as, and much more economical than, the traditional English turkey.

There is a delicious recipe for lemon chicken (although it makes a mess of the broiler). I serve it hot with a green side salad, but it is equally good cold. I once made it my basic dish for a picnic to watch the Oxford and Cambridge boat race in England: it poured with rain and the Cambridge crew sank – but the lemon chicken saved the day!

The recipe for chicken casseroled with lemon juice was supplied by the Holiday Inn in Amman. Easy to prepare, it can be made in advance of a dinner party.

Ferakh al-hara (hot chicken) is one of the easiest dishes to make in the book, an ideal recipe should you be eating alone after a busy day at work. I have a very "seasoned" palate, liking things hot, and tend to substitute chili powder for the sweeter paprika.

Cafés in Amman and Jerusalem are famous for chicken *musakhan,* a take–out snack like *döner kebap,* or *shawarma* as it is known in Arabic. *Sumak,* a red, crystalline spice with a lemony flavor, might be hard to find though.

As well as being masters at cooking chicken in so many different ways, Middle Eastern cooks take great pains to ensure that each dish has special eye appeal. Beautifully garnished with red paprika in oil and chopped walnuts, Circassian chicken is a good example. Side dishes are fluffy white rice and an emerald green salad.

Fesanjan, or tender duckling steeped in walnuts and pomegranates, is the king of all the poultry dishes. The medieval Persian recipe conjures up all the pomp and pageantry of the glorious reign of the Safavid *shahs.* If you can't find fresh pomegranate, use lemon juice or pomegranate juice concentrate, but the appearance of the dish will obviously suffer.

Restaurants in Lebanon have traditionally served small birds as *mezze.* Rubbed with salt, pepper and olive oil, they are grilled on skewers over a charcoal fire. A restaurant in the mountain town of Bhamdoun was famous for birds served in this manner. In Egypt, migrating quail are netted near Agami, a popular beach resort with Cairo's élite near Alexandria. Syrian farmers, especially around Aleppo, breed pigeons for the family pot.

Lemon Chicken Casserole

Serves 4-5:

*1 x 3 lbs chicken, or 2 small
    chickens
3 medium onions, chopped
3 cloves garlic, crushed
½ cup lemon juice
salt and pepper
2-3 tablespoons butter
a pinch of paprika
parsley, to garnish*

Skin and bone the chickens and cut the flesh into cubes. Mix these with the onions, garlic, lemon juice, salt and pepper in a large bowl. Cover, chill and marinate for 12 hours.

In a deep saucepan, sauté the chicken mixture in the butter, then add 1 cup of half water and lemon juice to taste. Cover and simmer on a low heat until tender, about 20 minutes. Serve with saffron rice, garnished with paprika and parsley.

*Lemon chicken casserole is
easy to prepare. A good recipe
for weight watchers.*

Chicken in Yoghurt

Serves 4:
1 stick butter
4 shallots, finely chopped
1 x 2½-3 lbs chicken, cut into
*   8 pieces*
a small bunch of parsley,
*   chopped*
1 teaspoon dried thyme
1 cup chicken broth
½ teaspoon salt
freshly ground black pepper
juice of 1 large lemon
2 teaspoons all-purpose flour
½ cup light cream
½ cup plain yoghurt

Melt the butter in a large deep skillet. Add the chicken pieces and cook, turning frequently, until golden brown on all sides, about 10–15 minutes. Add shallots, the parsley and thyme and cook until the shallots are transparent.

Add the broth, salt and lots of pepper, and simmer on a low heat for 30 minutes, turning the chicken pieces at intervals. If the sauce evaporates too quickly add a little of the lemon juice and some water.

Meanwhile preheat the oven to 450°F. Mix the flour with the cream, blend in the yoghurt and add the lemon juice.

Now grease a shallow ovenproof dish and place the chicken in it. Pour the sauce from the skillet into the cream mixture and blend slowly. Pour this mixture over the chicken and cook for 15 minutes. Reduce the heat to moderate, 350–375°F, and cook a further 15 minutes. Serve with puréed potatoes and a green salad.

Chicken in yoghurt sauce is an Egyptian favorite. Dip Arab bread in the sauce.

Ferakh al-hara *Hot Chicken*

Serves 4

*¼ cup plus 2 tablespoons
    olive oil
juice of 1 lemon
1 teaspoon chili powder
    to taste
salt and pepper
1 heaped teaspoon crushed
    garlic
1 x 2 lbs chicken, cut into 4
    pieces
lemon wedges, to garnish*

Preheat the oven to 375°F. Mix the oil, lemon juice, chili powder (or cayenne), salt, pepper and garlic in a bowl.

Place the chicken pieces in a baking dish and cover with the mixture. Bake for 15-20 minutes, basting occasionally. Do not baste for the final 15-20 minutes to allow the chicken to become crisp.

Serve with a rice *pilaf* and salad or as desired. Garnish with lemon wedges.

Ferakh al-hara or "hot chicken" can be made as hot as you want. Serve with plain rice and a green salad.

Chicken Musakhan

Serves 6:

*1 x 3 lbs chicken, cut into 6
   portions
2 cups chicken broth
1 small stalk of celery,
   including leaves
1 medium onion, sliced
salt and pepper
4 small onions sliced into fine
   rings
1 tablespoon pine nuts
1/4 cup oil
Arab bread, or pita bread per
   person
2 teaspoons sumak*

Place the chicken pieces in a casserole, cover with the broth and add the celery, the sliced onion and salt and pepper. Cover and simmer until tender, about 40 minutes. Remove the chicken and set aside a little of the broth. While the chicken is cooking, sauté the onion rings and pine nuts in the oil.

Arrange the bread on the broiler tray and top each piece with a portion of chicken, some of the onion rings and dribble a little broth over them. Sprinkle each with *sumak* and broil until the chicken turns golden brown. Take care not to burn the bread. Serve garnished with pine nuts and extra onion rings.

Musakhan can be eaten by itself, or with a salad. It is a novel ideal for lunch in the garden.

*Chicken musakhan is a
popular snack at cafes in
Amman. It is sprinkled with
sumak, a lemon-tasting spice.*

Persian Chicken

Serves 6:
2 medium onions, finely
   chopped
1 stick butter
¼ cup raisins
1 cup prunes, soaked, pitted
   and sliced
1 cup apricots, soaked and
   sliced
1 teaspoon ground cinnamon
salt and freshly ground black
   pepper
1 x 3-4 lbs fresh chicken

Sauté the onion in half the butter for a few minutes, then add the fruits and sauté gently for a further 5 minutes. Season the mixture with cinnamon, salt and pepper, and allow to cool.

Pre-heat the oven to 375°F while you are stuffing the chicken with the fruit mixture. Sew the neck flap to keep the moisture in. Rub all over with salt, pepper and remaining butter, wrap in foil and bake in the oven.

Open the foil after 40 minutes so the skin will brown and become crisp. The cooking time is approximately 1½-2 hours.

Stuffed with dried fruits, Persian chicken makes an unusual dish for a small dinner party.

Circassian Chicken

Serves 4-5:

1 x 3 lbs chicken
1 large onion, chopped
1 clove garlic, chopped
2 stalks celery, chopped
salt and freshly ground black
*   pepper*
1½ cups long-grain rice
½ cup plus 2 tablespoons
*   walnuts, finely ground*
3 tablespoons olive oil
1 teaspoon paprika

Put the chicken, onion, garlic, celery, salt and pepper in a large saucepan, cover with water and simmer until tender, about 1½ hours. Remove and drain the chicken (reserving the broth), and keep warm in a low oven.

Chill the broth quickly, then skim as much fat as possible off the surface.

Cook the rice (see pages 76-7), and keep warm in a low oven.

Meanwhile make the sauce. Put the ground walnuts in a deep skillet and add 1 cup of the broth. Bring to the boil, then simmer on a high heat, stirring until the mixture thickens. Season with more salt and pepper.

Now blend the oil and the paprika until the oil becomes bright red. Cut the chicken into attractive serving portions, arrange them on a bed of the rice. Cover with the sauce and trickle the red oil on top.

Circassian chicken makes an attractive presentation. Yoghurt and water is a common beverage in the Middle East. Also pictured are tomato and coriander salad and plain rice.

Roast Chicken stuffed with Rice and Pine Nuts

Serves 6:
1 large onion, finely chopped
1 stick melted butter
3 oz chicken livers, ground
½ lb sausage meat
¾ cup long-grain rice
¼ cup plus 2 tablespoons pine
    nuts
½ teaspoon ground cinnamon
¼ teaspoon allspice
salt and freshly ground black
    pepper
1 cup chicken broth
1 x 4 lbs fresh chicken

Using a deep skillet sauté the onion in two-thirds of the melted butter until it turns soft and golden. Add the liver and sausage meat and toss until lightly brown. Next add the rice, pine nuts, cinnamon, allspice, salt and pepper and cook about 5 minutes. To this add the broth and cook over a low heat until it is absorbed, about 12–15 minutes. Allow to cool.

Rub the entire chicken with salt and pepper. Spoon in the stuffing and close the openings with either small skewers or thread.

Brush with remaining melted butter and roast in a moderate oven (375°F) until the chicken is crisp and tender, about 2 hours. To crisp the skin, do not baste for the last 30 minutes.

Roast chicken with pine / nut stuffing will impress dinner guests.

Chicken Kebabs *(Cover)*

Serves 3-4

*1 x 2½-3 lbs chicken, boned
    and cut into good sized
    cubes*
½ cup olive oil
½ cup lemon juice
2 cloves garlic, crushed
*salt and freshly ground black
    pepper*
1 tablespoon melted butter
*saffron to color, or ½ teaspoon
    turmeric*

The chicken pieces should be of a size that will stay firmly on the skewers (leaving the skin on helps). Combine the oil, lemon juice, garlic, salt and pepper in a bowl, and place the chicken cubes in it. Cover and marinate for several hours, turning occasionally.

Dissolve the saffron or turmeric in the melted butter. Thread the chicken pieces on skewers and brush with this mixture. A charcoal fire or barbecue is ideal for cooking these chicken *kebabs*, but a good broiler is perfectly adequate. Cook over or under a high heat, turning and basting frequently with the butter, for about 15 minutes.

Serve the *kebabs* on the skewers on a bed of saffron rice (see page 76) garnished with sliced oranges. A plain lettuce salad would complement the meal nicely.

*Chicken kebab (cover).
Middle Eastern cooks pay
great attention to eye appeal.*

Broiled Lemon Chicken

Serves 6:

*2 x 2 lbs chickens, each cut
    into 6 pieces*
*1 large onion, very finely
    chopped*
juice of 2 large lemons
6 tablespoons peanut butter
¾ cup olive oil
salt to taste
freshly ground black pepper

Mix the onion, lemon juice, peanut butter,
oil, salt and pepper well and brush on the
chicken pieces. Place under a medium
broiler and cook until tender. Turn the
pieces and baste frequently with the
mixture, watching that it does not burn.
Serve when golden brown and tender.

   The chicken pieces may be eaten hot, or
cold, with a lettuce salad and rice *pilaf*.

*Peanut butter forms a
delicious crust on lemon
chicken. Excellent hot or cold.
An ideal picnic dish.*

Chicken with Olives

Serves 4:
1 chicken, about 3 lbs, cut into
   8 pieces
3 cups green olives, pitted and
   chopped
salt and pepper
3 cloves garlic, crushed
3 tablespoons olive oil
1 teaspoon freshly grated
   ginger
1 teaspoon turmeric, or 2-3
   strands of saffron
1½ cups chicken broth
1 teaspoon paprika
1 teaspoon ground cumin
½ cup lemon juice

Boil the chopped olives three times in a deep saucepan. Change the water on each occasion, except the last when you should use 1 cup of water with a pinch of salt. Remove from the stove and press the olives down with a potato masher to extract more juices. Set aside.

Sauté the garlic in the oil in a large, deep skillet. Add the ginger, turmeric or saffron, the chicken pieces and the broth. Cover and cook slowly on a medium heat, turning at intervals, about 30–40 minutes.

When the chicken is tender, remove it from the skillet and keep warm. Now reduce the broth until it becomes thick and pungent. Add the paprika, cumin, lemon juice and more salt and pepper according to taste. Simmer for a minute, then add the olives and their juices, stir well and allow the sauce to further thicken, about 12–15 minutes.

When ready to serve, place the chicken portions in the skillet and heat in the sauce. Serve each portion garnished with olives, with Arab bread to mop up the sauce, rice *pilaf* and chopped salad.

Braised chicken with olives.
Serve with rice pilaf and bread
to mop up the rich sauce.

Duck in Walnut and Pomegranate Sauce

Serves 4:
1 duck, about 4 lbs
salt and freshly ground black
pepper
2 tablespoons clarified butter
2 medium onions, chopped
½ cup plus two tablespoons
brown sugar
1 shallow teaspoon cinnamon
½ cup plus 3 tablespoons fresh
pomegranate juice, about 3
fruits (or grenadine syrup)
2 cups rich broth
1 cup finely ground walnuts

Garnish *(optional)*
1 cup coarsely chopped
1½ cups whole fresh
pomegranate seeds

Rub the duck well with salt and pepper. Melt the butter in a deep skillet and brown the duck on all sides. Remove and keep warm in a low oven (about 300°F).

Drain the excess fat from the skillet and sauté the onion until soft and transparent. Add the sugar, cinnamon, pomegranate juice and broth, stir well and simmer uncovered for about 12 minutes.

Remove the duck from the oven and turn the heat to 425°F. Melt a little butter in a baking dish, then replace the duck in the oven. After 10 minutes, drain off excess fat and reduce the oven to moderate (375°F).

Now spoon half the quantity of sweet sauce over the duck and continue to baste frequently except for the final 30 minutes of cooking. Turn only once during this time, after about 1½ hours. Drain the fat as it exudes out of the duck and separates

from the sauce.

When the duck is nearly cooked, add the finely chopped walnuts to the remaining sauce in the skillet, adjust the seasoning as necessary, stir well, simmer on a low heat, 5-10 minutes, and keep warm.

Continue to drain excess fat off the duck, being careful not to waste any of the sauce. The skin should turn a crisp, rosy brown.

There are two options when serving *fesanjan*. For eye appeal, present the duck whole, garnished with the sauce, the chopped walnuts and pomegranate seeds. Alternatively carve it, and pour the sauce over each serving. You can also leave the sauce for people to help themselves. Serve with *chelo* (see page 76) and a lettuce salad.

Seafood

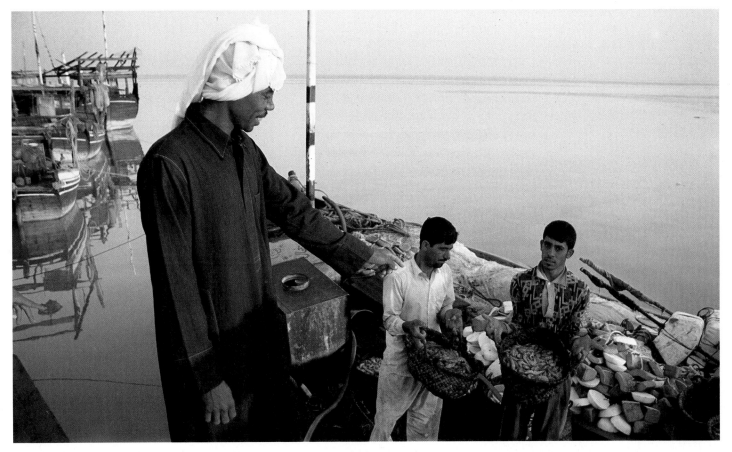

Buying the family fish in Bahrain. The Arabian Gulf is renowned for excellent seafood.

Some of my most memorable meals in the Middle East have been seafood – but then I love fish. The setting of many seafood restaurants is also a bonus. How could I forget grilled fish by the creaking water wheels on the Orontes river at Hama, in Syria?

There is a restaurant near the Roman city of Jerash, in Jordan, which serves wonderful grilled perch – known locally as St Peter's fish – from the Sea of Galilee. More rustic is a restaurant in Aqaba with *al fresco* tables under half a dozen straggly palms. The fish is good – you choose your own in the kitchen – but the smell of the charcoal grill attracts Aqaba's 100,000 cats who practically drag it off your table.

Baghdad is famous for open-air restaurants serving *mashgouf* or smoked fish along the banks of the Tigris. The Iraqis do interesting things with fish, especially in the delta port of Basra, but some of the best seafood dishes are found in the Arabian Gulf. Despite oil spillages, the tepid waters of the Gulf abound in seafood: fish, crab, giant prawns and a delicately flavored, flat-chested cousin of the lobster known as *Umm Robien*.

Hotels have a field day with such a variety of fish. No one chooses smoked Scottish salmon from the Bahrain Hilton buffet, but the local prawns, crayfish and cold cod disappear in minutes.

The early morning fish markets of Manama, capital of Bahrain, Kuwait, Dubai and the other Gulf states are a hive of activity the moment the *dhows* unload. In

Muscat, capital of the Sultanate of Oman, sardines and other fish are sold straight from smaller boats known as *houris*.

The Red Sea off Yemen and Saudi Arabia is equally rich in fish: barracuda, bass, cod, lobster and crabs. While the *Quran* imposes no dietary restrictions, shellfish are avoided by many Muslims, a parallel with Judaic dietary laws which forbid eating any fish without fins or scales.

And while the Mediterranean lapping southern Europe grows daily more toxic, the Eastern Mediterranean and the Aegean supply Turkey, Syria and Lebanon with a veritable treasure trove of seafood. One of the many delights of Istanbul is lunch at a sunny seafood restaurant beneath the Galatea Bridge linking the European and Asian sides of the city. At night seafood restaurants along the Bosphorus are packed.

The world's finest caviar comes from the Caspian Sea in northern Iran. The sturgeon are netted as they congregate to spawn and the eggs are scooped from the living fish. During travels around the Caspian Sea, I ate beluga caviar daily for lunch, with a raw onion, lemon, salty butter and local bread. Then back in Tehran, I enjoyed beluga caviar with sour cream and *blinis*.

The most popular eating fish in the Middle East are red mullet (known by the grand title of *Sultan Ibrahim* in Arabic), *arous,* a fish like the French *daurade* or silver bream, sole, bass, tuna and turbot down to sardines.

Among freshwater fish, the *chahoute* (similar to a trout) is netted in the Tigris-Euphrates river systems in Iraq. This is the famous *mashgouf* which is cleaned, split, staked and smoked around an open fire. Pungent and tender, it is impossible to copy in a kitchen. In Basra and the Arabian Gulf States, fish baked in date purée is popular.

Tuna and swordfish *kebabs* are a speciality of Turkey where coastal restaurants also serve stuffed mussels and squid. *Samak mashi* or stuffed fish, fish baked in *tahini* sauce and baked fish eaten with *muhammara* are common in Syria and Lebanon. Arabs eat basically the same fish dishes, although an Indian influence has made seafood curries equally popular. Nile fish tend to taste muddy, but there are good seafood restaurants in Suez and Alexandria, *saadiyeh,* or plain fish and rice, and grilled or fried small fish being common dishes.

Some Middle Eastern countries still enjoy traditional dried, salted fish. A common sight in Dhofar, in southern Oman, are sheets of silver sardines drying along the beaches.

Wasif, tiny fish like sprats, are salted and dried by fishermen on the Tihama coast of North Yemen. Trucked to the mountain towns, they are sold by the basketful in local souqs. The fish adds zest to *zahawiq,* a popular Yemeni dip made from tomatoes and chilis.

Essentials for cooking fish the Middle Eastern way are plenty of olive oil, lemon and cumin. Skewers are needed for *kebab*-style fish while a double-sided broiler is useful. The two sides secure the fish so that it is easily turned over the fire, or under the broiler.

Cold Fish in Olive Oil

Serves 4:

1 x 2 lbs whole fish (cod, bass, mackerel or similar)

½ cup olive oil

1 large sweet green pepper, seeded and finely chopped

2 medium onions, sliced

3 cloves garlic, crushed

6 medium tomatoes, peeled and sliced (or 14oz can)

1 tablespoon tomato paste

a bunch of parsley, finely chopped

salt and pepper

lemon wedges and 12 green or black olives, to garnish

Wash and clean the fish of any loose scales and pat dry on a paper towel. If the skin is thick, make several incisions to aid cooking. Heat the oil in a large pan and fry the fish slowly, cooking lightly on both sides (about 10 minutes). Lift out gently, drain on paper towels and allow to cool.

Sauté the green pepper in the same oil, then add the onion after 5 minutes and cook until both are soft. Add the garlic and sauté for a further 2 minutes. Pulp the tomatoes and blend with the paste and parsley. Add to the pan, season to taste, stir well and simmer for 15 minutes.

Lift the fish carefully back into the pan, cover with the sauce and cook gently for 10-15 minutes. If the sauce is too thick, add a little water mixed with lemon juice.

Finally, remove the fish to a large serving dish and pour the sauce over it. Surround it with the olives and lemon wedges, cool and then refrigerate. Remove about 10 minutes before eating.

Cold fish salad is ideal for a summer buffet table.

Crayfish Tail Curry

This recipe is based on a popular dish made from *Umm Robien,* **a type of lobster found in the Arabian Gulf. It can be adapted to shrimps, crayfish or other shellfish.**

Serves 4:
4 medium crayfish, about 1 lb each
3 tablespoons olive oil
juice of 1 large lemon
1 bay leaf
2 cloves garlic, crushed
3 medium onions, sliced
1 celery stalk
2 tablespoons clarified butter
1 inch fresh root ginger, peeled and grated
1 level teaspoon turmeric
1 teaspoon ground coriander
1/2 teaspoon ground cumin
1/2 teaspoon chili powder
1 heaped tablespoon shredded coconut
4 medium tomatoes, skinned and chopped (or 1 small can with juice)
salt and black pepper
freshly chopped coriander, to garnish

First prepare the crayfish tails: shell and chop into chunks, then marinate in olive oil and some of the lemon juice with seasoning for 2 hours. Cover broken shells with cold water, add some onion, a bay leaf, celery stalk and salt and pepper. Simmer until you have a rich, aromatic broth. Strain well and set aside.

In a deep skillet, sauté the garlic and remaining onion in the clarified butter until soft and transparent. Add the spices and coconut and sizzle for 1 minute.

Now add the tomato and remaining lemon juice and cook for 10 minutes, stirring well. Stir in the broth, marinade and crayfish tails, and simmer uncovered until the tails are tender and the sauce is reduced, about 15-20 minutes.

Garnish with finely chopped coriander leaves and serve with rice *pilaf.*

Crayfish tail curry from the United Arab Emirates has a hint of India. Use any long-tailed crustacean.

Fried Fish

Serves 4:

8 small fish (fresh sardines or herrings)
4 cloves garlic, finely chopped
½ teaspoon ground cumin
salt and white pepper
2 tablespoons finely chopped parsley
all-purpose flour
cooking oil
sliced lemon and tomato, to garnish

Wash and clean the fish under running water, then pat dry on paper towels.

Mix the garlic, cumin, salt and pepper and parsley and rub over the fish inside and out. Cover and chill for 1 hour so the fish will absorb the flavors.

Now roll each fish in the flour. Heat enough oil to semi deep fry the fish. When it is sizzling hot, slip each fish in and cook quickly on both sides, about 10 minutes. Serve garnished with lemon and tomato.

Prawns in Tomato Sauce

Serves 4:

2 lbs prawns
1/2 teaspoon ground cinnamon
salt and freshly ground pepper
3 cloves garlic, crushed
2 medium onions, finely
     chopped
2 tablespoons oil
1/4 cup tomato paste
5 medium ripe tomatoes,
     peeled, chopped and puréed
1/4 cup lemon juice
freshly chopped parsley

Shell the prawns. Wash and dry them, then season with the cinnamon, salt and pepper.

Sauté the garlic and onions in the oil until they are soft. Blend in the tomato paste diluted with a little water. Add this to the pan mixture and mix in the fresh tomato purée, stirring well. Allow to simmer on a gentle heat, about 12 minutes.

Add the prawns and cook on a medium to high heat for about 10 minutes. Stir frequently and remove from heat when tender. Sprinkle with lemon juice and parsley and serve on a bed of plain rice.

Prawns in tomato sauce. The Arab states are renowned for king-size prawns. This recipe is from Saudi Arabia.

Baked Fish with Saffron Rice

Serves 4:

1 large whole fish (such as bass, or cod), about 4lb
3 cloves garlic, crushed
olive oil
fresh lemon juice
salt and freshly ground black pepper
1 large tomato, sliced
1 lemon, sliced
1 recipe Saffron Rice (see page 76)
lemon wedges and parsley, to garnish

Wash and clean the fish under running water and pat it dry with paper towels. Rub over inside and out with a mixture of garlic, oil, lemon juice, salt and pepper. Place the tomato and lemon slices inside the fish, skewer or sew to hold together, and chill for 2 hours.

Place the fish in a large, greased baking dish and cook in a moderately hot oven – 375°F–400°F until the flesh is tender and the skin is golden brown (about 40–50 minutes).

Serve on a bed of saffron rice and garnished with lemon wedges and parsley.

Baked fish served on saffron rice is the most common way of cooking fish.

Barbecued Fish with Dates

Serves 4:

1 cup dried, pitted dates
4 whole white fish, about ¾lb
  each
salt and pepper
2 medium onions, finely
  chopped
1 clove garlic, crushed
½ teaspoon turmeric
a generous pinch each of
  ground cumin, coriander,
  cardamom, nutmeg and
  cloves

Soak the dates in cold water until they become soft – about 4 hours.   Choose fresh fish. Gut and rinse the cavities well under cold running water. Do not scale. Dry the cavities with paper towels and sprinkle with a little salt and pepper.

Mix the onion, garlic and spices with a little water and stuff each fish with this, securing the cavities with threads, or small skewers.

Now make a purée of the dates. Drain them, then blend with a little water, or put through a sieve. Blend just long enough to

obtain a soft paste, then smear this on both sides of each fish. Cook over a charcoal fire, about 5 minutes each side. Test with a fork to make sure the flesh is tender. A double wire grill is useful for this dish.

Serve hot with a rice dish. The skin together with the scales can be peeled off when eating. The date purée gives the flesh a pleasant nutty flavor.

Fish in Hot Sauce

Serves 4:
4 cloves garlic, chopped
1½ teaspoons ground
    coriander
4 thick fillets white fish, about
    ¾lb each
2 tablespoons olive oil
1 tablespoon lemon juice
salt and white pepper
lemon slices, to garnish

Sauce
½ stick butter
½ small sweet red pepper,
    diced
4 medium tomatoes, skinned
    and chopped
1 large onion, diced
1 teaspoon paprika
½ teaspoon ground ginger
a pinch of salt and pepper
1 tablespoon tomato paste
    mixed with a little water

Pound the garlic and coriander together in a pestle and mortar. Rub this into the fish fillets and chill in a covered bowl for 2 hours.

Heat the oven to 375°F. Remove the fish from the bowl and rub with a mixture of the oil, lemon juice, salt and pepper. Lay the fillets in a flat, oiled baking dish, cover tightly with foil and bake for about 20–30 minutes.

Meanwhile, prepare the sauce. Melt the butter in a skillet and sauté the pepper, tomato and onion until soft. Add the seasonings and the tomato paste and mix well. Simmer for 10–15 minutes on a low heat.

Serve the fish in the baking dish, garnished with the hot sauce and lemon slices.

In the Levant, fish fillets or whole fish are baked and eaten with *muhammara* as a side dip. Some people even spread it over their fish.

Baked Fish in Tahini Sauce

Serves 4:
*1 whole white fish, about
  2½ lbs, or fillets according
  to the number of guests
salt and pepper
½ cup olive oil
juice of 2 large lemons
½ cup tahini (sesame
  seed paste)
1 large onion, chopped
parsley, to garnish*

Gut, scale and clean fish under running
water. Dry, and sprinkle with lemon juice.
Chill for 2 hours. Remove to room
temperature and rub with salt, pepper and
some of the oil. Bake at 400°F, about 20
minutes, or until tender. While the fish
cooks, sauté the onion in the remaining oil.

Meanwhile blend the *tahini* and lemon
juice, adding water to achieve a creamy
sauce. Remove the fish from the oven,
sprinkle with the onions and coat with the
tahini sauce. Return to the oven and bake a
further 10 minutes. Garnish with parsley and
serve with rice and a salad.

Tuna Shashlik

Serves 4:
1 lb tuna or firm game fish
2 lemons
10 bay leaves
4 tablespoons olive oil
salt and pepper
8 cherry tomatoes
a bunch of fresh thyme
5-6 small white onions

Skin and bone the tuna and cut into chunks. Put into a bowl with the juice of 1 lemon, the bay leaves and the oil. Grind black pepper over it, mix well and marinate for 1 hour, turning frequently.

Meanwhile wash the tomatoes. Make a small incision in the tops and squeeze out the seeds. Insert a drop of oil, salt and a leaf of thyme in each.

Slice the second lemon. Thread the fish, the onions, tomatoes, bay leaves and lemon slices alternately on a skewer. Pour the remaining marinade over it and season with salt and pepper.

Broil under a high heat until cooked – about 10 minutes – then serve immediately with rice *pilaf* and a green salad.

Tuna shashlik is eaten with rice. Skewered fish is popular in the Eastern Mediterranean and in Egypt.

Stuffed Squid

Serves 4 *as a main course with salads etc.*

6 medium squid (about 6
    inches when whole)
¼ cup plus 2 tablespoons
    olive oil
¼ cup plus 2 tablespoons
    thick tomato juice, or 2
    medium tomatoes, skinned
    and pulped
salt and pepper
a pinch of paprika
juice of 1 lemon

Stuffing
2 medium onions, finely
    chopped
4 tablespoons olive oil
chopped arms of squid
¼ cup plus 2 tablespoons rice
1 tablespoon of either dill
    weed or mint, finely
    chopped
2 tablespoons parsley, finely
    chopped
1 tablespoon pine nuts
a pinch of ground cumin

To clean the squid, hold the body in one hand and gently pull off the head and arms: if done correctly, the body contents should come away as well. Clean the body thoroughly under cold running water, discarding anything left inside, including cartilage etc. Rub off any pigmentation from the body and set aside. Chop off the arms and put aside for the stuffing. Discard the heads.

In a glass bowl, mix the olive oil, the tomato juice, salt, pepper and paprika. Place the squids in this mixture, coat well and leave to marinate while you make the stuffing.

In a deep skillet, sauté the onions in the oil until soft. Add the chopped arms and cook with the onion until they change color. Now add the rice, dill or mint, parsley, pine nuts and cumin and cook 5-10 minutes, stirring with a wooden spoon. Leave to cool.

Remove the squids from the marinade and partly fill each one with some of the stuffing. Allow room for the rice to swell during cooking. Secure the opening of each body with cocktail sticks, or thread.

Arrange the squid in a lightly oiled baking dish, cover with the marinade, the lemon juice and enough boiling water to almost cover them. Bake about 50 minutes in a hot oven 400°F until tender. Serve cold.

Stuffed squid are worth the preparation. Serve with a salad and bread to mop up any sauce. Tiny grilled squid are sometimes served in a mezze.

Desserts and Sweetmeats

The oldest known Islamic sweetmeat is *faludhaj,* a Persian concoction of ground almonds, sugar, rose water and other ingredients, which is believed to have been introduced in Mecca to cater for pilgrims making the *haj* or pilgrimage.

Ancient Arab and Farsi records make little reference to other rich desserts, but the Muslim sweet tooth can be traced back at least as far as the Abbasid caliphate. Recipe books from this period indicate that Abbasid society was addicted to sweetmeats, a taste not restricted to affluent families.

Among a variety of rich sweetmeats were *lawzinia* (a confection of almonds, breadcrumbs and syrup), *zalabiya* (an almond and rose water flavored tart) and *khabis* which seems to have resembled a type of gelatine made with breadcrumbs, milk, sugar and sesame seed oil. Sugar, honey, molasses and syrup were commonly used sweeteners. Many people in the Middle East still believe that eating honey and other sweet things will ward off the "evil eye".

Sweets figure in many prominent dates in the Muslim calendar. Prior to *Muharram* (the first ten days of the New Year) or on the Prophet's birthday, housewives are busy cooking traditional sweetmeats. It is a custom to take these to relatives and friends who similarly call with their own homemade specialties.

Baklava is probably the best known sweetmeat. I have eaten *baklava* in places as far apart as Dakar and Sydney – wherever

Baking biscuits in Baghdad, center of Islam under the Abbasid caliphs. Many recipes originate from this period.

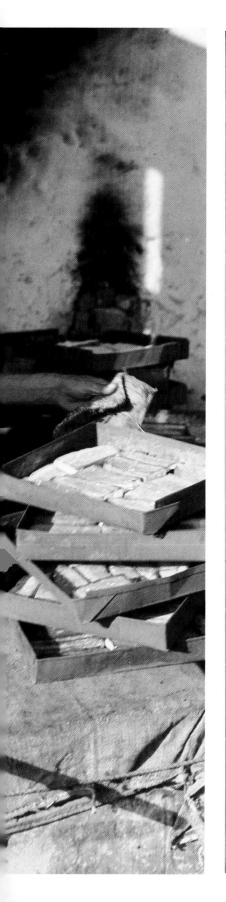

there are Lebanese, Turkish or Armenian migrants. The Greeks also claim it is their own invention, but its true origins are obscure. *Baklava* keeps quite well, but it is best eaten within a day or two of preparation. It can be made using either walnuts or pistachio nuts.

Basbousa is another syrupy sweetmeat which can be made with yoghurt or coconut. It may be eaten hot or cold, with or without cream.

There can be few people who have never tasted *lokum,* or Turkish delight as it is more commonly known. Many restaurants habitually offer a dish with coffee. I have not supplied a recipe for Turkish Delight as it can be readily bought and it is *so* time consuming to prepare. Also served with coffee are delicate almond fingers, a truly magical sweetmeat which I have enjoyed in many Middle Eastern homes.

Ma'moul are bite-sized pastries of many different shapes and fillings. Outside the great Ummayad Mosque in Damascus is a shop selling them oven-warm. You can buy a bag for under a dollar to eat as you wander through the bazaar, one of the biggest and most interesting in the Middle East.

Dates have a myriad uses in Middle Eastern cookery. The Bedouin often eat them with bread and yoghurt as a substantial meal. They can be stuffed with marzipan or puréed to give a nutty flavour to fish. Tribes in remote parts of Saudi Arabia sustain their camels on date meal.

While the West Bank town of Jericho is more famous for citrus fruits, bananas also flourish in the almost semi-tropical climate of the Jordan Valley trench. Plantations can be seen on either side of the River Jordan and after the harvest bananas hang side by side with oranges and grapefruit in Jericho's roadside stalls. Banana cake or banana loaf is an old Palestinian recipe, sometimes sold in shops, more often made at home.

Recipes appear for three glorious Middle Eastern desserts. My own favorite, *ma'mounia* or "Caliph's Delight", is a recipe said to have been created for the Caliph Ma'moun. A speciality of the Syrian town of Aleppo, it is often eaten for breakfast smothered in cream. Local folklore says it assists a woman to regain her strength after childbirth – what it does for men being something of a moot point. Similar to the drier *basbousa,* which is also made from farina, *ma'mounia* is extravagantly rich.

Made from ground rice, *muhallabia* is to the Middle East what rice pudding is to England or America. A very simply, delicately flavored dish, it is eaten throughout the region, then under the name of *firni,* it pops up in Pakistan having probably been introduced by invading Mughals.

Umm Ali, or "Mother of Ali", is a very rich pudding, very fattening and utterly irresistible if you have a sweet tooth. Dried fruit salad can be made with many different combinations of dried fruits and nuts. It is served when Muslims break the fast at dusk. Eat it with cream and be sure to make enough to have on breakfast cereal – it's delicious.

"Caliph's Delight"

Serves 6:
2 cups water
juice of 1 lemon
1 cup (white) sugar
1 stick butter
¼ cup pine nuts
¾ cup semolina
ground cinnamon
heavy cream

Combine the water, lemon juice and sugar in a saucepan, bring to the boil and simmer for 15 minutes.

In a large skillet, melt the butter and lightly sauté the pine nuts. Add the semolina and cook on a low heat until the semolina turns light brown, about 5 minutes.

Remove from the heat and stir in the syrup. Return to a low heat, stir well and cook for a further 5 minutes. Transfer the mixture to a serving dish and serve sprinkled with cinnamon and heavy cream. It may also be eaten cold.

Umm Ali *"Mother of Ali"*

Serves 6:
10oz cooked puff pastry
¼-½ cup pistachio nuts,
    chopped
¼-½ cup flaked almonds,
    toasted
2 tablespoons lemon juice
1 cup milk
¾ cup sugar
a pinch of cinnamon
1 egg, beaten
2 teaspoons rose water
1 cup light cream

Grease a round, glass baking dish, and preheat the oven to 375°F. Crumble the pastry into the dish and mix with the nuts and lemon juice.

Heat the milk, sugar and cinnamon to just below boiling point, then slowly add the beaten egg. Pour this over the pastry mixture in the dish, and sprinkle with rose water. Top with the cream and bake for about 30 minutes, until golden.

Umm Ali is a very rich dessert made from flaky pastry, nuts and cream.

Muhallabia *Ground Rice Pudding*

Serves 6:
5 cups milk
3 tablespoons ground rice
1 tablespoon corn starch
6 tablespoons sugar
1 tablespoon rose water
½ cup ground almonds
chopped almonds (or
    pistachio nuts) and freshly
    grated nutmeg, to garnish

With a little of the milk, mix the ground rice and cornstarch to a smooth paste.

Slowly heat the sugar in the rest of the milk, and add the rice paste, stirring continuously with a wooden spoon. Simmer the mixture until just below boiling point, and take care not to let it burn on the bottom as this will spoil the delicate flavor. The mixture should thicken in about 15 minutes.

Add the rose water and ground almonds and continue stirring in one direction on a low heat. Simmer for a further 5 minutes, then remove from the heat and cool slightly before pouring the mixture into an attractive glass bowl, or individual glass dishes.

Garnish with almonds or pastachio nuts, and sprinkle with the nutmeg. Leave to chill for about 3–4 hours before serving.

Made from ground rice, muhallabia is the most common dessert in the Middle East. Rose water gives it an Oriental touch.

Banana Loaf

1 stick butter
¼ cup plus 2 tablespoons
    sugar
2 eggs
a pinch of cinnamon
1 teaspoon vanilla extract
3 medium ripe bananas
¼ cup walnuts, coarsely
    chopped
1¼ cups all-purpose flour
2 teaspoons baking powder
1 teaspoon bicarbonate soda
a pinch of salt
1 tablespoon milk

Cream the butter and sugar together, then add the eggs, one at a time, beating after each addition. Add the cinnamon and vanilla and beat well.

Mash the bananas to a pulp, then stir into the mixture together with the walnuts. Combine well, then fold in the sifted dry ingredients alternating with the milk.

Pour into a greased 9 x 12 inch loaf pan lined with waxed paper and bake for 45 minutes in a moderately hot oven 350–375°F.

Simple, almost Western, banana loaf from Palestine. Cook with or without walnuts and spread with butter according to taste.

Date Rolls

Makes about 24 rolls:

1 cup plus 2 tablespoons
all-purpose flour
1 stick less 1 tablespoon sweet
butter, softened
1 tablespoon powdered sugar
1 tablespoon oil
2 tablespoons milk

Filling

2 tablespoons butter
2 tablespoons water
1½ cups dates, pitted and
chopped

Make the filling first. Melt the butter together with the water in a saucepan, then add the chopped dates. Cook on a low heat, stirring the dates and pressing down until they become a soft paste. Remove and cool.

To make the dough, sift the flour into a mixing bowl. Cut the soft butter into small pieces and work it into the flour with your fingers. Add the sugar and mix in thoroughly. Make a well in the center, pour in the oil and milk, then continue to knead the dough until pieces flake off the sides of the bowl. Knead a further 10 minutes, then roll into a ball and chill.

Now preheat the oven to 350°F and grease a large baking tray. Remove the dough from the refrigerator and divide into three portions. Knead each well.

On a floured board roll out and flatten a ball of dough. Cut into a neat rectangle shape. Spread one-third of the date mixture thinly over the top. Roll the rectangle into a roll and continue to roll backwards and forwards until it grows longer and thinner. Slice this into flat, diagonal sections, about 1½ inches thick. Repeat this process using the remaining balls of dough.

Place all the slices side by side on the greased baking sheet and prick the tops lightly with a fork. Bake for 25-30 minutes in the pre-heated oven until slightly colored (if you overcook them, they become hard). Allow to cool, then dust with powdered sugar.

Baklava

1lb filo pastry (about 20
 sheets)
about 1 cup sweet butter,
 melted
1 cup chopped pistachio
 nuts or walnuts
1 teaspoon ground cinnamon
2 tablespoons sugar

Syrup
2¼ cups sugar
¼ cup honey
2 cups water
1 tablespoon lemon juice
1 tablespoon orange blossom
 water

Make the syrup first to give it time to chill.
Dissolve all the ingredients together over a
medium heat. Remove from the stove
when the mixture thickens enough to coat
a spoon, cool, then chill thoroughly.

Grease the base and sides of a large
baking pan about 13 x 9 x 2 inches.
Layer it with 9 sheets of pastry, brushing
each sheet with melted butter.

Mix the nuts, cinnamon and sugar and
spread half over the top filo sheet.
Place 2 more buttered sheets on top, and
cover with the rest of the nuts. Layer up the
remaining filo sheets, brushing each with
butter as before. Crimp the edges of the
pastry and with a sharp knife, cut a
diamond pattern in the top. Sprinkle with
water to prevent the top layers of pastry
from curling.

Bake for 30 minutes in a moderate oven
350°F. Increase to hot 425°F and bake for a
further 10–15 minutes, until the pastry is
puffy and the top is gold. If the top layer
cooks too quickly, cover it with foil, but do
ensure that the pastry is cooked right
through.

Take the *baklava* from the oven and pour
the very cold syrup over the hot pastry.
Leave to cool. When it is cold, cut into
small diamonds or squares and serve.

Above right   *The king of
sweetmeats, baklava has
Turkish origins.*

Right   *Basbousa is one of
many Middle Eastern
sweetmeats made from farina.
Ideal to serve at afternoon tea.*

Basbousa with Coconut

Syrup

1 cup sugar
lump of jaggery (if available)
1 tablespoon lemon juice
1 cup plus 2 tablespoons
  boiling water

Mixture

1 stick butter
1½ cups farina
¾ cup sugar
½ cup shredded coconut
½ cup all-purpose flour
½ cup milk
1 teaspoon baking power
a few drops of vanilla extract
12 blanched almonds

First make the syrup by dissolving the sugar (and jaggery, if used) in lemon juice and boiling water. Simmer until it thickens, then allow to cool.

To make the "cake" melt the butter, then pour into a large mixing bowl. Mix in all the other ingredients, and stir well with a wooden spoon. Spoon this mixture into a shallow, 12 inch baking pan and flatten the top well.

Bake in a moderately hot oven 375°F for about 30 minutes, or until it turns golden. Remove and cut into diamond shapes, placing half an almond on each piece. Pour over half the syrup and bake for a further 5 minutes or until golden brown (do not burn the almonds). Serve warm with the rest of the syrup.

Basbousa are usually eaten hot, but they are also delicious eaten cold. They will keep fresh for several days.

Ramadan Dessert *Dried Fruit Salad*

Serves 10:

Soak all the dried fruit overnight. Measures are for soaked fruits.

1 cup dried apricots
1 cup dried prunes
1 cup mixed dried fruits with peel (raisins, currants, candied orange peel)
1 cup raisins
4 chopped dried figs (optional)
3 cups water
½ cup sugar
1 cup mixed nuts (pine nuts, walnuts, almonds), chopped
light cream
grated nutmeg

Bring the water and sugar to the boil in a large saucepan. Stir 15-20 minutes, or until it becomes a syrupy consistency. Add all the fruits and simmer 1½-2 hours. After 1 hour add the nuts and mix well.

Remove the mixture from the heat and allow to cool before refrigeration. Serve in a cut glass bowl or individual dishes. Pour light cream over the top and garnish with grated nutmeg.

Ramadan dessert is eaten when the Muslim fast is over at dusk.

Stuffed Dates

1lb fresh dates, pitted
Almond Paste
¾ cup blanched almonds
1 large egg white
1 cup plus 2 tablespoons
    powdered sugar
2 teaspoons almond extract
2 drops rose water
food coloring, as desired

Spread the almonds on a baking sheet and place in a slow oven 325°F for 10 minutes, or until they are oily, but not brown. Allow to cool, then grind in a food processor.

Add the egg white, sugar and almond extract, and process until the consistency of paste. Add rose water and coloring as desired, and blend briefly. Chill overnight.

Turn the paste into a small bowl, break off small lumps and stuff each date.

Stuffed dates are made on special occasions such as the eid al-fitr holiday. Iraq and Oman produce the best quality dates.

Almond Fingers

Makes about 30 fingers:
12 sheets filo pastry
¼ cup sweet butter
¼ cup sugar
½ cup plus 2 tablespoons
  finely ground almonds
a pinch of ground cinnamon
1 teaspoon rose water
powdered sugar, to garnish

Slice each pastry sheet into three rectangles. Brush each rectangle with the melted butter.

Mix the sugar, the nuts, cinnamon and rose water together, and place about a teaspoon of this in the center of each rectangle. Fold the sides in and roll into a cigar shape.

Place in rows on a greased baking sheet and cook for 30 minutes in a moderate oven 325–350°F, or until the pastry turns pale gold. Remove, cool and dust with powdered sugar.

Almond fingers are dainty sweetmeats dating from medieval times.

Orange Slices with Cinnamon

Serves 4:

Choose navel oranges if possible. Peel and slice 3 oranges thinly, removing any pith and seeds. Arrange on a glass dish and sprinkle with ground cinnamon. Chill, then remove from the refrigerator 10 minutes before serving.

Figs with Orange Juice

Serves 4:

This is a simple dessert which can be prepared in advance. Cut the stalks off about twelve fresh figs, but do not peel them. Quarter them and arrange in a flower effect on a dish. Cover with orange juice and chill.

Date and Banana Dessert

Serves 4:
1lb fresh, pitted dates
4 bananas
1 cup light cream
*¼ cup roughly chopped
   walnuts*
nutmeg

Fill either a glass bowl or individual glass dishes with alternate layers of sliced dates and bananas. The dates should be as fresh as possible and the bananas on the greener side.

Cover with cream and chill for at least 2 hours so the dates will absorb the cream.

Garnish with walnuts and freshly grated nutmeg.

Easy to prepare chilled desserts: figs with orange juice (above left), cinnamon orange slices (above right), and date and banana (below).

Next page   A selection of typically Middle Eastern fruits.

Beverages

Alcohol is forbidden by the *Quran*. This is not to say that several countries do not produce some palatable wines: Turkey, Syria and Lebanon are wine producers and to a lesser extent, Egypt. The fiery aperitif *arak* is drunk in the Levant. The Turks drink it throughout the *mezze*, in fact a *mezze* without *arak* (or *rakı*) is unthinkable.

Muslim families commonly drink mineral water or soft drinks with their meals. Lebanon bottles mineral water, and the tiny Gulf emirate of Ajman supplies the whole of Arabia with fine mineral water from an inland spring.

The ringing of the water seller's bell is still a familiar sound throughout the Middle East and in Egypt in particular. The bearer of news, the water seller has an important rank in street society. In the old days other street vendors used to sell fruit juices from glass flasks strapped onto their backs; today rows of juicers whizz in sidewalk cafés. Only in poor rural communities will you find someone still squeezing oranges, or pressing sugar cane on a crude machine salvaged from automobile parts.

Fresh lemon, or better still fresh lime juice, is my favorite beverage on a hot day. In 1964, after traveling across North Africa, I spent some time staying with my cousin who worked at the British Embassy in Cairo. Each afternoon, an old lime seller used to call at her flat in Zamalek and on hearing his call from the street below, she would lower a basket for limes for our gin and tonics. And I particularly remember a tangy *limoonada* which revived me after a morning spent photographing the ruins of Persepolis, in Iran.

The ancient Persians were masters at making effervescent *sharbats* or sherbets from oranges, limes, apricots and other fruits. The pomegranate is a favorite fruit in Iran – it is said that the Prophet Muhammed urged his followers to eat it because it purged the system of envy and hatred. Using vivid metaphors, poets from Ferdowsi to the present day have compared the pomegranate to a women's womb, ripe with progeny, to young maiden's cheeks and the opened fruit to a broken heart, the seeds like tears of blood.

Tamarind juice is another popular beverage, especially in Syria and Iraq. The drink of nomads, yoghurt and water is commonly drunk with meals in Turkey and Yemen. Crushed almonds and milk is the stuff of the "Arabian Nights".

Tea spiced with ginger and cinnamon is popular, but coffee, and the making and serving of coffee, has pride of place in Middle Eastern folklore, the whole coffee ritual being like a silent language that binds both host and guest.

In traditional Bedouin society, a guest is invited to take his place around the fire in the men's section of the tent. The host then digs into the coffee-bag and puts some beans in a ladle to roast on the embers. When they have cooled, he pounds them with a pestle and mortar or *mihbash* of traditional carved wood, or brass.

A skilful coffee grinder can

The Middle Eastern coffee ceremony is like a silent language binding both host and guest. Twigs act as a filter in the spout. Photographed in Wadi Rum, Jordan.

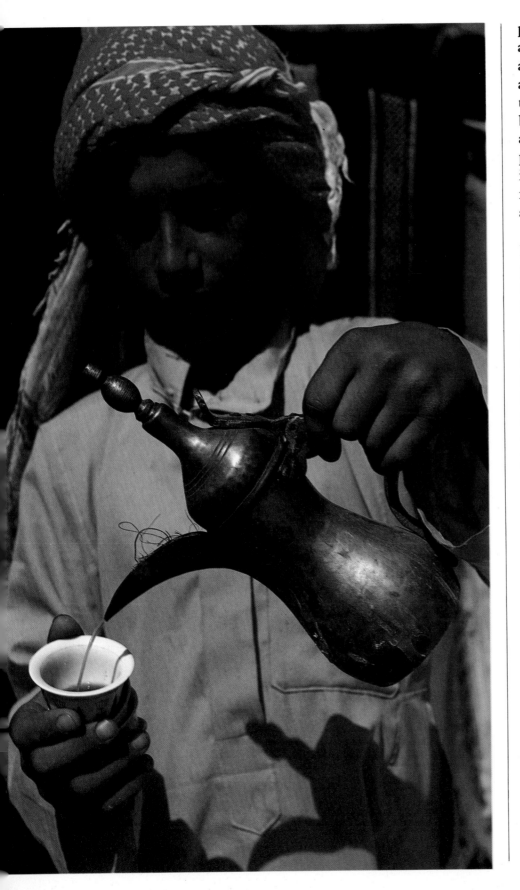

pound out an appreciable rhythm audible at some distance, announcing to neighbors the arrival of a guest. The beans are tossed into boiling water and after boiling several times, the contents are poured into another pot and a pinch of freshly ground cardamom is added. This is allowed to simmer for about 15 minutes, the pleasant aroma pervading the whole tent.

The following gestures, now largely symbolic, remain essential protocol in the basic Bedouin coffee ceremony of the Middle East.

The first cup, offered to the host, is deemed the "unworthy cup"; assuring the guest that the coffee is safe to drink and confirming to the host that it is hot, since it is a terrible insult to serve cold coffee. Like the other cups, the second cup is poured with the left hand, the bearer palming the tiny white china cups in his right. This cup is offered to the guest whose acceptance signifies that he is pleased with the hospitality.

The third cup, even more significantly, has its roots in the days of tribal feuds. It silently concludes the protection agreement, meaning that the guest is safe from any attack while under the auspices of his host. This cup, known as the "sword cup", is binding, even against attack by one or the other's relatives. Sometimes a fourth cup is offered, confirming the silent defense pact.

It is not usual to drink more than this, but if a guest wants more (only a few drops are poured into each cup) he simply holds out his cup to be refilled by the attentive bearer.

Alternatively, to signify he has had enough, he flicks the cup a couple of times with his wrist, the final concluding gesture to the coffee ritual.

Unfortunately, "Turkish coffee" as it is known in the West, is growing rare. High prices on the world coffee bean market have put many Middle Eastern coffee houses out of business and in Mocha, the famous coffee port in North Yemen, there is not even a drop of Nescafé! Chasing the quick profits from *qat*, local farmers have torn out their traditional coffee bushes and instead planted *Catha edulis (qat)*.

Qahwa (Arabic for coffee) uses coffee grounds and cardamom pods in varying quantities. It is served at every opportunity. You can be seated only seconds in someone's home or office when, like a genie (or *djinn* in Arabic), a bearer arrives with a pot of *qahwa* and a stack of tiny cups.

I especially recall an early morning in Dubai when I drove into the desert to watch Bedouin training a young falcon. Seated in their tent, I was invited to share their humble breakfast of bread, sandy dates and *qahwa*. No race is more hospitable than the Bedouin who will go without rather than have nothing to offer.

Yoghurt Drink

Serves 8:
6 cups plain yoghurt
6 cups ice water
1 tablespoon finely
  chopped fresh mint
a pinch of salt

Mix all the ingredients together, then garnish each glass with a little extra mint. Using seltzer instead of water makes an even more refreshing drink. Serve well chilled.

Yoghurt drink (above left) is especially popular in Iran and Turkey. Almond drink (above right) echoes the "Arabian Nights".

Almond Drink

Serves 6:
1 cup blanched almonds
sugar, to taste
1½ cups water
3 cups milk
1 teaspoon orange blossom
  water
a few drops of almond extract

Chop the almonds and combine in a blender with the sugar and water. Blend until smooth, then add the remaining ingredients. Garnish with a rose petal.

Middle Eastern Lemonade

Serves 6:

8 lemons
¾ cup sugar, or to taste
1 teaspoon orange blossom
    water, or to taste
generous ¼ cup freshly
    chopped mint
water (or seltzer) and ice
    cubes

Squeeze the juice from the lemons and sweeten to taste with the sugar. Add the orange blossom water and the mint, and stir or shake well together. Pour a little into a tall glass and fill with water or soda and ice.

Popular thirst quenchers throughout the Middle East are lemon, orange and colorful pomegranate juice.

Orange Sharbat

Serves 6:

16 medium oranges
sugar to taste
1 teaspoon orange blossom
    water
water (or seltzer) and ice cubes
sprigs of fresh mint, to garnish

Squeeze the juice from the oranges and sweeten to taste with the sugar. Add the orange blossom water and mix well. Serve diluted with ice cold water and garnished with mint.

Pomegranate Drink

Serves 4-6:
3 cups fresh pomegranate juice
½ cup fresh lemon juice
1 teaspoon orange blossom
    water
sugar to taste
a pinch of salt
seltzer or water, to taste, and
    ice cubes

Combine everything in a blender, or mix well in a pitcher and serve with ice cubes.

Turkish Coffee

There are three ways of ordering coffee in Arabic, and these are: sweet (*helou* or *sukkar ziada*), medium (*mazbout*) or unsweetened (*murra*). Sugar is boiled with the coffee and the quantity will depend on the preference of your guests. This recipe is for medium coffee, to give an idea of the sugar quantities. If other guests require *helou* coffee, or no sugar at all, then you must brew another pot. Even if you like ordinary coffee without sugar, it is rare to drink Turkish coffee, as it is so sharp, without some sweetening.

Serves 2:
4 tablespoons roasted ground coffee
1 heaped teaspoon sugar
2 small coffee cups water
a tiny pinch of ground cardamom

Combine all the ingredients in a long handled coffee pot or tiny saucepan, stir well and bring to the boil. As the froth forms on top, remove from the stove, stir again and return to the heat until the froth rises again. Be very careful it does not boil over. Boil it briefly again, then stand aside for a few seconds.

Have the small cups ready to pour in the coffee, raising the pot (difficult with a saucepan) to get a nice head of froth on each cup. The grounds should be allowed to settle a minute or two before the coffee is drunk.

Rose Petal Tea

Serves 4:
1½ cups rose petals
3 cups water
honey to taste

Choose fresh rose petals. Strip the flower gently under running water then place the petals in a saucepan. Cover with the water and boil for 5 minutes, or until the petals become discolored. Strain into teacups and add honey to taste.

Qahwa *Arab Coffee*

Serves 6:
6 cardamom pods
¾ cup cold water
1 heaped tablespoon dark roast coffee, coarsely ground

Turkish coffee (left), rose petal tea (center) and qahwa (right). Turkish coffee is dark and strong. Qahwa is rather bitter. All are common hot beverages throughout the Middle East.

Bruise the cardamom pods by pounding gently in a pestle and mortar. Using a long handled coffee pot (or a tiny saucepan), place in it the water, pods and coffee. Bring to the boil, then simmer on a low heat for 15 minutes until the grounds settle.

Serve *qahwa* in tiny white coffee cups – Arabic ones do not have handles – about 2 tablespoons in each. *Qahwa* is not served with sugar, and its rather bitter flavor is not to everyone's taste. It is traditional Arabic coffee.

Index

Measures

All measures in this book are American, so here are a few conversions for non-American readers.

A large (1 kg/2 lbs) loaf tin is similar to a 9 × 5 × 3 inch loaf pan, while a small (500 g/1 lb) loaf tin is similar to a 4½ × 2½ × 1½ inch loaf pan.

All cup and spoon measures are level unless otherwise indicated.

The imperial pint is 20 fl oz whereas the American pint is 16 fl oz. The British standard tablespoon holds 17.7 ml whereas the American tablespoon holds 14.2 ml.

American	British
1 tablespoon or 3 teaspoons	1 tablespoon
2 tablespoons	1½ tablespoons
3 tablespoons	2 tablespoons
¼ cup	3 tablespoons (2 fl oz)
⅓ cup	4 tablespoons
6 tablespoons	5 tablespoons
½ cup	6 tablespoons (4 fl oz)
⅔ cup	¼ pint
¾ cup	6 fl oz
1 cup (8 fl oz)	scant ½ pint
1¼ cups	½ pint
2 cups (1 US pint)	¾ pint
2½ cups	1 pint

Spice Names

The following are Arabic translations of the most commonly used spices — a handy guide for shopping in the *souqs:*

Allspice: *bahar*
Anise: *anisun*
Black Pepper: *fil-fil afwad*
Cardamom: *hayl (habahan)*
Chili: *fil-fil ahmar har*
Cloves: *kabsh qaranful*
Coriander: *kusbarah*
Cumin: *kammun*
Fenugreek: *helba*
Ginger: *zanjibil*
Mace: *fuljan*
Nutmeg: *jawz al-teeb*
Paprika: *fil-fil ahmar*
Saffron: *za'fran*
Sesame seed: *sim-sim*
Tamarind: *tammar al-Hindi*
Tumeric: *kurkum*

Acknowledgements

I would like to thank Gulf Air, the national carrier of Bahrain, Qatar, the United Arab Emirates and the Sultanate of Oman for helping with this project. Gulf Air is the only Middle Eastern airline member of the Chaine des Rôtisseurs: Gulf seafood, dates and Arab coffee are local delicacies on their menu. I would also like to thank the Bahrain and Kuwait Hiltons for their hospitality. All the Middle East Hiltons are renowned for excellent food, ethnic buffets being a special feature. The Sheraton Hotel in Sana'a was most helpful during difficult research in North Yemen. In London, Barbara Tobias, Aileen Aitken, Joan Parker, Raghad Ahmed, Abdul Latif Salazar, Akın Urs and other friends were especially encouraging. Special thanks, go to my editor, Susan Fleming, home economist Norma Miller, and to Multimedia's Chief Editor, Anne Cope. Part of the introduction to the Beverages section is reproduced from my book *An Insight and Guide to Jordan* published by Longman (1981).

CHRISTINE OSBORNE

PICTURE CREDITS